The Northern Line

Mike Horne a...
Bob Bayma...

UNDERGROUND

Capital Transport

First published 1990
Second edition 1999

ISBN 185414 208 9

Published in association with the Northern Line, London Underground Ltd,
by Capital Transport Publishing, 38 Long Elmes, Harrow Weald, Middlesex

Printed by CS Graphics, Singapore

© Mike Horne and Bob Bayman 1990, 1999

This edition combines material published in the books 'The First Tube' (1990) and
'The Northern Line' (1987) with additional material to bring the story up to date.

The front cover painting is by Peter Green, GRA

The maps are by Mike Harris

The back cover poster is copyright London Transport Museum

CONTENTS

Artist's impression of the crossover at the Stockwell terminus of the original City & South London Railway. Printz Holman

London Before the Tubes

Today, the Greater London Area occupies 610 square miles, and most of it is substantially built upon. But 150 years ago London was little bigger than the area presently enclosed within London Underground's Circle Line, which is a mere 6¾ square miles. It had taken several hundred years before that to expand from the walled City of London, only one square mile in size. An important part in this phenomenal expansion during the twentieth century was played by the newly developed tube railways.

Although tiny by modern standards, the rapidly expanding London of 1840 was creating mounting communication difficulties. It must be borne in mind that both the electric telegraph and telephone were yet to be introduced. The penny post had only arrived that year and it was only eleven years previously that the first London 'omnibus' service began, though the proliferation of these horse-drawn vehicles did not by any means solve the growing transport problem, being inherently slow and contributing further to the congestion in the almost medieval streets.

Traffic congestion has kept road speed to around 10mph in central London since the 1850s. This scene shows the Bank junction at the turn of the century. Guildhall Library

The arrival of the main line railways from the 1830s had further contributed to the mounting chaos, having been obliged to stop at London's outskirts, at Paddington, Euston and King's Cross, although those on the south and east were later to penetrate slightly further into the centre. Although the art of 'commuting' was virtually unknown, the arrival of the railways began to bring the home counties within easy access of London, and a country home became a practical possibility – not that it was to remain country for long.

Numerous schemes were proposed to ease the problem. London was expanding at an increasing pace and the problems of travel were getting worse, with journeys becoming longer as well as more numerous. After several years of argument it was agreed to build a railway beneath street level, connecting the main line termini together and bringing a railway into the City of London itself. This became the Metropolitan Railway and opened in 1863 from Paddington to Farringdon Street, via Edgware Road, Baker Street, Portland Road, Gower Street and King's Cross.

The Metropolitan Railway was a milestone in London's transport history. Although it was built to Brunel's broad gauge (7 feet) and used steam locomotion, it was novel in that much of it ran under the ground within tunnel (or, more strictly, a covered way). Construction was immensely disruptive. First a vast ditch had to be excavated, the walls of which were then lined with bricks. Then the roof had to be erected and the ground made good above. Although substantial demolition was required, the method of construction generally dictated that the line ran beneath the roadway, where the inconvenience caused to frontagers was considerable and, of course, the road had temporarily to be closed while work took place.

By 1884 a completely circular underground railway had been built (now the Circle Line) and numerous extensions made into the emergent London Suburbs – though the extensions were almost all of the conventional type, either at or above ground level. The last short links of this circle had cost a hugely disproportionate amount to finance and it was becoming clear that on grounds of both expense and inconvenience these shallow underground railways could never penetrate into modern central London. Another answer had to be found.

The answer came almost by chance – it was literally lateral thinking. Whilst the Metropolitan Railway was being built an engineer named Peter Barlow was sinking vertical cast iron cylinders into the Thames at Lambeth as part of the pier foundations for a suspension bridge (opened in 1863). It occurred to Barlow that cast-iron tunnels of similar construction could just as easily be driven horizontally under the river with perfect safety, and he subsequently advocated that such tunnels could be used as 'omnibus subways for the relief of traffic congestion in London'. In succeeding years others were also to contemplate the theme of pipes or tubes, but by digging a trench and inserting a pipe (or caisson) then covering it over. Only a small and short-lived, pneumatically-powered mail-conveying scheme between Euston and Holborn (opened in 1865) was in any way even a partial success and two passenger carrying schemes failed to come to fruition. These also would have required major surface works along their routes.

But Barlow pursued a different approach. He wanted to construct his iron-lined tunnels from beneath the ground. He adapted a concept used many years earlier by Sir Marc Brunel, that of using a massive shield at the working face to protect the workmen and to hold back the ground until the permanent tunnel had been erected. Barlow's shield was first patented in 1864; it was to be circular and propelled forward by screw jacks, pushing against the completed tunnel behind.

Barlow was first able to apply an improved version of his invention in London, on a short subway beneath the Thames near the Tower of London. The ¼-mile subway was authorised by Act of Parliament in 1868 and opened in August 1870. The tunnel consisted of flanged segments bolted together and had an effective internal diameter of only 6ft 7¾ins. For around 100ft under the Thames the tunnel was level, but at each end it rose at 1:29 to the stations. Track was 2ft 6ins diameter carrying a single cable-hauled car attached by a gripper to a steel-hauled cable driven by steam engines. At the two stations the shafts were equipped with lifts; passengers were conveyed at a small charge (one penny second class and twopence first).

The mechanical equipment was unreliable and the venture was a commercial failure with the receivers arriving in only three months. The equipment was stripped in December 1870 and the tunnel was relegated to pedestrian use until public closure in 1896 when the new Tower Bridge rendered it unnecessary. In civil engineering terms, however, the scheme amply demonstrated the potential of this form of tunnelling. Three factors emerged. First, a form of tunnelling now existed which was particularly well suited to the blue clay which lies in a fairly uniform stratum beneath much of London; this also permitted construction below many of the existing pipes and sewers of the City. Secondly, it was now possible to build a railway whose construction needed only a limited number of surface access shafts and entirely avoided the massive scale of disruption caused by the arrival of the Metropolitan Railway. Thirdly, it reduced the amount of expensive land required, improving the economics of the whole operation. London was now free to enjoy a railway more or less anywhere it was wanted.

The massive disruption caused while building the shallow covered ways of the Metropolitan Railway was virtually unavoidable. LT Museum

The Pioneer Tube

The engineering success of the Tower Subway encouraged Barlow to propose another, much larger, cross-river scheme in 1870 – the Southwark & City Subway. This would have been about 1.3 miles long, running between the City and St George's Church, Southwark. Mindful, no doubt, of the poor financial results of the Tower Subway backing was not forthcoming and the proposal could not be pursued. Nevertheless, later developments eventually caused the idea to be revived, and in 1884 an Act of Parliament authorised a modified and renamed City & Southwark Subway between a point in the City (by the Monument) and the Elephant & Castle. Barlow was considerably aided by a former pupil of his, James Greathead, who designed the tunnelling shields required.

Tunnelling started in October 1886. The work began from a shaft sunk into the river at the Old Swan Pier, just upstream of London Bridge. Additional working shafts were built at station sites along the line of route. The tunnels were to be larger than those on the Tower Subway, at 10ft 2ins (internal). This time the tunnelling shield was driven forward by means of hydraulic jacks, a method which has been adopted ever since. From the initial shaft in the river, twin tunnels were driven towards each terminus, a separate tunnel for each direction of traffic. Like the Tower Subway it was intended that the carriages be hauled by means of cable traction (which was by then in use on some tramways). This involved continuously driven cables to which the cars could clamp themselves by means of mechanical grippers, controlled by the drivers. The engine house was planned to be at Elephant & Castle.

By the time construction was in hand, further consideration had been given to the route of the line and it had been decided to extend further south, to salubrious Stockwell, for which powers were granted in 1887. A less tortuous alignment was chosen for this portion, allowing plans to be considered for cables operating at 12 mph, against the 10 mph of the northern section. With this in mind, a slightly larger tunnel diameter was also chosen – 10ft 6ins – though of course the carriages would still be constrained by the smaller northern tunnels.

It was during construction that some serious worries about the method of propulsion began to emerge – the operational problems looked increasingly formidable. Matters were not helped by the failure of the cable company with which the Subway was associated. In the light of these developments the Subway looked with mounting interest at the few pioneer electric systems then in operation. This led to the taking of a very brave decision, particularly in view of the infancy of the electrical industry of the day, and the pursuit of cable operation was abandoned.

After much investigation the company was finally persuaded to employ Messrs Mather & Platt as electrical contractors, their chief engineer, Dr Edward Hopkinson, having had much experience with pioneer electrical traction on the Bessbrook & Newry Tramway in Ireland. John Hopkinson (Edward's brother) was employed as consulting engineer for the project. From 1888 the Subway took all necessary steps to facilitate the use of electrical traction, and was considerably reassured by some

Stockwell station, 4th November 1890, as the Prince of Wales arrives for the official opening and the first royal journey by tube railway. LT Museum

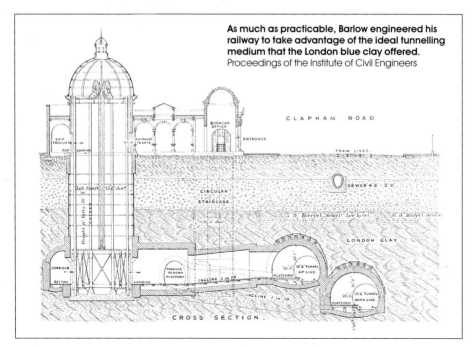

As much as practicable, Barlow engineered his railway to take advantage of the ideal tunnelling medium that the London blue clay offered.
Proceedings of the Institute of Civil Engineers

successful experimental running in September 1889 using temporary generators installed at Borough. Two experimental carriages were delivered by Ashbury's and brought down the lift shaft in a dismantled state to gain access to the track; a prototype locomotive came the same way, and was later joined by a second one. The first loco had the motors mounted directly on the axles while on the other one the axles were driven via gearing, which proved unnecessarily noisy. In the event twelve production locomotives were ordered (thus making 14 in all) using the direct drive approach, but a little heavier than the prototype of that ilk.

It was unfortunate that the initial proposal for cable haulage, and various construction expediencies, meant that some parts of the new line were not entirely suitable for the use of electric locomotives; restrictive tunnel diameter, sharp curves and steep gradients being the major difficulties. Nevertheless the line opened under the revised name of the City & South London Railway and thereby had the honour of being the first major electric railway in England.

The formal opening took place on 4th November 1890 and was performed by the Prince of Wales (subsequently King Edward VII) although public services did not begin until Thursday 18th December. By modern standards the railway was crude and primitive. By the standards of the day it was a leap into the future. The small electric locomotives were generally effective in hauling their three diminutive carriages at an acceptable speed and without the curse of the steam and smoke which pervaded the older Metropolitan and District Railways.

The line was about 3½ miles from end to end. Each intermediate station (Borough, Elephant & Castle, Kennington and Oval) had a separate platform for each track. At the City (called King William Street) there was a single track with a platform each side, while at Stockwell there was an single platform with a track each side. Although the running tunnels were of cast iron and circular, the 200ft long station platforms were of brick and the lower portion was flattened off, to avoid wasted space.

C&SLR Carriage No.30. The short wheelbase and the long bogie frames carrying the separate gated vestibule are clearly seen. The very small windows, and the cushioned interior of the carriages, gave rise to the nickname of 'Padded Cells'. This carriage is now in the LT Museum. LT Museum

1897 and King William Street station is decorated for **Queen Victoria's Diamond Jubilee.** Beneath the flags a notice proclaims 'To the Oval in Ten Minutes' – a time unmatched by the traffic-encumbered horse-bus. Guildhall Library

Apart from King William Street where an existing building was adapted, the remaining stations were of an attractive design by T P Figgis and each incorporated a large dome above the lift shaft (though the hydraulic equipment was at the bottom of the shafts).

Like the modern Victoria Line, the City & South London Railway (C&SLR) was entirely underground except for the depot near Stockwell station. This was located just east of the Clapham Road, and consisted of carriage and locomotive sheds and sidings. It was connected to the railway by a long inclined tunnel at the steep gradient of 1 in $3\frac{1}{2}$ and up which the trains were hauled by a rope. After a very few years this tunnel went out of favour – a feeling perhaps fuelled by a runaway train which then derailed and wrecked itself – and it was replaced by a large lift which brought the locomotives and carriages to and from the surface one at a time. To ease matters, a complex of sidings was built at the lower level and much maintenance was done there without the need to bring the carriages to the top level.

The power station was also on the depot site and hydraulic pressure was created here for conveying in a hydraulic main to the stations for operation of the station lifts. The electrical equipment was installed by Mather & Platt Limited of Manchester and comprised three (soon four) Edison-Hopkinson dynamos powered by 375hp Fowler Engines. It should be recalled that large-scale electricity generation was very much in its infancy in London and not only was Stockwell the first large-scale generating station to supply a traction load but was, when opened, the largest generating plant in London. No substations were provided, the power being fed directly to the conductor rails.

Because the railway was fed only at the southern end there was frequently a substantial voltage drop at the City, to be something a problem on the steeply inclined approach to King William Street. Contemporary reports suggest that not all trains managed to get up this incline at the first attempt and accordingly trains had to set back and take a run at it, sometimes more than once; it is recorded that even on those trains which did make it the lighting in the carriages faded to a dim red glow. Several attempts were made to improve on the situation, even to the extent of saving electricity on the station lighting circuits by using the emergency gas lights as the normal source of illumination.

The method of electric operation chosen involved a three rail electric traction system at 450 volts dc, with the conductor rail mounted between the standard gauge running rails and supported on glass insulators. The conductor rail had to be mounted off-centre to avoid fouling equipment, and the top surface was below running rail level, requiring the locomotive pick-up shoes to be raised by moveable wooden ramps at pointwork, which was something of a complication.

On the locomotives a form of control known as series/parallel operation was adopted (patented by John Hopkinson in 1887) with accelerating resistances being switched out directly by a hand operated controller. The Westinghouse air brake system was used but the locomotives were not provided with air compressors to supply the braking system; the reservoirs had therefore to be recharged once on every round trip at Stockwell.

At the opening of the line there were 30 carriages built by the Ashbury Carriage & Wagon Company. These wooden-bodied carriages sought to provide an adequate level of comfort even despite the lack of window space, not that there was much to look at outside. Each vehicle could seat 32 people; the seat risers were formed out of the steel underframing, behind which the wheels were allowed to protrude above the floor level. The seats were therefore all longitudinal with the backs built into the body shell and carried up to within six inches of the roof, where narrow frosted windows were provided. Access was gained from the ends, where gated gangways gave access to station platforms, the landings being supervised by assistant guards, later styled 'gatemen'.

One of the original C&SLR locomotives, No.10, in later modified form outside Stockwell depot. The piping from the roof carries the air brake across to the adjacent carriage. LT Museum

A contemporary wash drawing illustrating the station at King William Street (C&SLR) in the period 1890-95. The platform on the left is used for departure traffic and the other for those arriving. The layout was adjusted such that in the period from 1895 until closure in 1900 there were two tracks with a single island platform between.

The signalling system was essentially of a conventional mechanical nature, although with a novel form of 'Lock and Block' control superimposed where an electrical detector proved a train to have left the section before the following one could be signalled forward. Signal cabins were provided at all stations and at Borough, Kennington and Oval the differences in platform level meant a separate cabin was needed on each platform. The signals themselves were semaphores at stations, while in the running tunnels the restricted space meant that mechanically operated lamp signals were used.

When the railway opened, passengers entered and left the system through turnstiles, at entry paying a member of staff a flat fare of twopence – though no tickets were issued. This system lasted less than a year as traffic patterns required the railway to try a variety of fares depending on time of day and location, though without tickets fares from any one station at any one time had to cover every destination. Tickets made their inevitable debut from 1892, for selective return fares at first, but by the time the railway expanded graduated fares with tickets were introduced for all journeys and the turnstiles abandoned.

As a deep level tube railway the C&SLR was an engineering success. As an electric railway, it was a triumph too. There *were* problems. The brick station construction led to some subsidence (and was not repeated) and the electricity upset some delicate measurements at Greenwich Observatory, some five miles away. But these were trifles compared with the arrival of a clean, new and, above all, successful new system of transportation which was to transform travel patterns in London over the next century.

The City & South London Grows

The little railway was now to pay the penalty for being a pioneer. The tiny tunnels and the struggling electrical supply were problems enough, together with under-powered locomotives and the limitations of the block signalling arrangements with station-to-station sections. Locomotive operation presented other line capacity constraints too; at each end of the journey the incoming locomotive had to be uncoupled from the train and a replacement coupled up at the 'outgoing' end of the train, with accompanying shunting moves and delay. Then there were the cramped and dingy carriages, reputed to ride rather roughly. Nor did the layout at the north end of the line – set out for cable operation – prove at all satisfactory with the alignment of the station hardly lending itself to future expansion of the line. In exasperation the layout of King William Street was altered in 1895 to give a twin track arrangement with an island platform between, though this did make it quite impossible to run trains of more than the prevailing three carriages.

With great determination the C&SLR got to grips with these shortcomings and made what improvements it could. Meanwhile traffic levels responded and services were further improved. Seven further locomotives were constructed by various manufacturers in the period to 1899; these bore certain differences to the first batch although they were substantially similar. Fifty-four further coaches were delivered during the same period, once again very similar but incorporating proper windows (later at least some of the padded cells were reconstructed to incorporate windows). The power supply was also improved by further re-arrangements in 1895 and 1896. The line capacity was enhanced by the introduction of additional home signals which allowed the block sections to be shortened.

Plans were soon made for a northerly extension of the line to Islington, but after much debate the only feasible arrangement demanded that the near mile-long section from King William Street to a point just north of Borough be abandoned and replaced by new under-river tunnels and a new station at Bank. Parliamentary powers were obtained for the extension and other works in 1893, and included the diversion from Borough. Stations were to be constructed at London Bridge (irritatingly not served on the old route), Bank, Moorgate Street (now Moorgate), Old Street, City Road and Angel.

The new portion of the line opened as far as a temporary terminus at Moorgate Street on Sunday 25th February 1900. Each of the three new stations was constructed in twin large-diameter cast-iron tunnels lined with white tiles, and access from the surface to lower levels was achieved by means of electric lifts (first tried at Kennington in 1898). At Bank land values were understandably high, and the company made arrangements to construct a sub-surface ticket hall based on an enlargement of the crypt of St Mary Woolnoth church. Unfortunately it became necessary for massive underpinning work to be done as the fabric of the church was found to be less substantial than originally thought. Although the work was eventually completed with entire technical satisfaction it became necessary for the sum of £170,000 to be paid to

With a platform 40ft by 10ft and rated for loads of up to 16 tons, the Stockwell carriage lift could convey either locomotives or carriages the 60 feet from surface to tunnel level. The carriage is one of a post-1890 batch with slightly larger windows. The spiral staircase runs down the edge of the oval liftshaft. LT Museum

King William Street disused station in 1939. Although platforms and track have been removed, the signal box (and signals) are intact, together with gas lights. During the Second World War this station was converted into an air raid shelter. LT Museum

the church authorities by way of compensation, though not until the railway had unsuccessfully taken matters to the House of Lords.

The new surface station at Moorgate Street was an impressive building and when the extension opened the company removed their office there. Interchange was available at Moorgate with the Metropolitan Railway, and at Bank with the Central London Railway. A crossover and siding was built at London Bridge (originally to have been called Denman Street), and an emergency loco spur at Moorgate Street, also equipped with a scissors crossover with the signal box mounted above. Once the former City terminus had been jettisoned it became possible to start operating 4-coach trains with immediate traffic relief.

The remainder of the Islington extension opened on 17th November 1901 with intermediate stations at Old Street and City Road. The latter station was built with separate platform tunnels while Angel was built with an island platform in a single large diameter tunnel. Electric lifts were provided at both stations. All the new running tunnels were built at an 11ft 6ins diameter. At Angel and Old Street sidings long enough to hold a complete train were built.

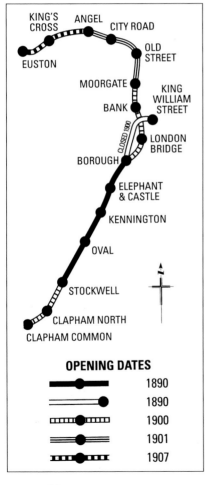

OPENING DATES

●———	1890
═══●	1890
▭▭▭●▭▭▭	1900
═══●═══	1901
▪▪▪●▪▪▪	1907

Left **Map showing C&SLR opening dates (modern names used for clarity). The sharp curve at the northern end of the original line followed the curve of Arthur Street directly above. This was necessary to avoid going under property.**

Below **Moorgate station in 1914. This building became the headquarters of the C&SLR.** LT Museum

The removal of the King William Street bottleneck at last allowed of a modest southerly extension too. Powers had been obtained for this as long previously as 1890, but it was feared that without an increase in capacity further north the line would not be able to cope. Extension work began in 1898 and the new route opened in 1900 with stations at Clapham Road (now Clapham North) and Clapham Common. The platform tunnels at both consisted of a single 29ft 8ins diameter tunnel with an island platform flanked by the two tracks; the running tunnel diameter was 10ft 6ins. Again, electric lifts connected the lower station levels with the new surface buildings. The extension came into use on 3rd June 1900.

The Stockwell power house and the power supply systems were totally unsuitable for the expanded railway and a new power house was built nearby with a capacity of 3.25 megawatts, the former building being converted into repair shops. The railway was nervous about alternating current distribution even though it was adopted on the Central London Railway which opened in July 1900. A 5-wire dc distribution system was thus adopted (another invention of John Hopkinson) with 2000 volts between the outer conductors, and 1000 volts between the inner conductors. This arrangement caused the conductor rails on each track to be of opposite polarities, one being 500 volts above and the other 500 volts below earth, with the track rails earthed. At the termini all tracks necessarily had to be on the same polarity, and a 30ft dead section was installed on the approach line where current rail polarity was reversed. Motor-generator 'boosters' were provided at London Bridge and Angel (the equivalent of substations), with motor-generator 'balancers' at Clapham Common, Elephant & Castle and Moorgate Street – these latter sought to balance the voltage on each track when unequal loads were drawn. Large battery banks were also installed at Stockwell and Angel to provide some emergency backup in the event of power failure, and also to supplement the supply during very heavy demand.

With the abandonment of the former City terminus it became possible to operate four-car trains. The additional rolling stock this required was built by several manufacturers, these cars being constructed by G.F.Milnes & Company. The design was a modified version of the original stock. M.A.C.Horne Collection

Drawing of the original depot at Stockwell.
M.A.C.Horne Collection

By 1902 the locomotive stock had risen to 52, with some of the older locomotives having been rebuilt and modernised; the new locomotives were of a more powerful type, built by Cromptons. Further coaches were also purchased, increasing the coaching stock to 140; the new coaches were similar in principle to the older batches, with wooden construction on a steel underframe continued, though detailed changes – to the windows for example – were made. These substantial increases in rolling stock were justified by the equally substantial increases in traffic; nearly 13½ million passengers being carried in 1901 compared with just over 5¼ million in 1891.

The final extension of this railway, while still an independent concern, was in 1907 when it pushed farther north to tap the main line traffic at King's Cross, St Pancras and Euston. At platform level Euston was very much like Angel, being accommodated in a large single tunnel, whilst at street level there was an ornate station building in Eversholt Street. In addition there was direct access to the main line station via an additional ticket hall (initially staffed by the main line company) beneath the main concourse, which entrance also served another new tube line (described later). Each booking hall had its own separate electric lifts which led to opposite ends of the new platform. At King's Cross – the only intermediate station – there were separate tunnels with the station lifts coming down between the platforms, the lift landings being conveniently placed at platform level. At top level there was a ticket hall beneath the forecourt of King's Cross, but with a subway leading to St Pancras station. Between Angel and King's Cross an intermediate signal cabin was required and a subterranean cabin with surface access from Weston Street (now Weston Rise) was provided, together with a dip in each track – still detectable today – to assist trains to restart. Running tunnels were constructed at 10ft 6ins diameter.

The extension opened on 12th May 1907. A further 25 coaches were provided to service the extension and permit other improvements, this time of steel-bodied construction but otherwise generally similar to their predecessors, though perhaps more plush; by now 165 carriages had been built and all trains were operated as 5-coach sets. A novel feature at Euston was the provision of an engine traverser in a connecting tunnel just north of the station, to aid the process of locomotives running round; this facility appears to have been short-lived. A scissors crossover and siding were provided just south of Euston.

Some additional generating plant was installed at Stockwell, and some direct feeders from Angel booster station to King's Cross, but no new boosters or balancers were felt necessary. The signalling was to the same standard as elsewhere on the line.

A rare (and posed) photograph of the C&SLR below ground prior to reconstruction. Taken at Euston, one of the later batches of locomotives is evident in the platform on the left and a train of the more recent rolling stock on the right. The entrance to the train through the gated platform between the carriages is clearly visible and may be seen to be a single vestibule between them, unlike the Hampstead cars where there were separate platforms on each car. The platform on the right now forms platform 6 at Euston. NRM

The ornate C&SLR surface building at Euston was closed in 1914, despite dating from only 1907, when facilities were concentrated in the ticket hall beneath the London & North Western Railway station. LT Museum

The Hampstead Tube

The technical success of the City & South London Railway soon caused a number of schemes to be put forward for further tube railways in London. One of the quickest off the mark was the Hampstead, St Pancras & Charing Cross Railway, the Parliamentary Bill for which was just one of many such tube railway bills presented to the 1892 parliamentary session. It contemplated a railway between a point under the junction of Southampton Street and Strand, via Charing Cross Road, Tottenham Court Road, Hampstead Road, thence Camden High Road and Chalk Farm Road, Haverstock Hill to a point under the junction of Heath Street and High Street at Hampstead. A branch was proposed diverging eastwards at the Euston Road and running under Drummond Street to Euston and King's Cross.

Parliament established a committee to examine the various Bills; it reported favourably on the Hampstead scheme, resulting in the Royal Assent being given on 24th August 1893 – the proposed line having become known as the Charing Cross, Euston & Hampstead Railway in the meantime, and with the section from Euston to King's Cross being truncated east of Chalton Street. Stations were to be built at Hampstead, Belsize Park, Chalk Farm, Seymour Street, Euston Road, Oxford Street, Charing Cross and Euston. A station was also contemplated at Camden Town, but was initially less certain. It might be noted that the proposed Seymour Street station was not actually in that road at all (it was at the junction of Camden High Road, Hampstead Road and Eversholt Street – Seymour Street was somewhat farther south). At Charing Cross the station was to be linked to the South Eastern Railway terminus though the tracks themselves were to lay beneath the Strand, in the direction of the City (this was later changed such that they pointed towards Hungerford Bridge).

Difficulty was found in procuring the necessary share capital (to become a recurrent theme) and the directors had to be content with keeping the scheme alive rather than in actual construction. Several further Acts succeeded in preserving the powers but made some detail changes, including incorporating Euston on the main line (rather than a branch), and building a new branch from Camden Town to Kentish Town (Midland) railway station and thence to a depot and power station a little farther north. By now electric operation was clearly intended, although when first mooted it was felt that the gradients would demand cable haulage. Powers were again renewed in 1900 but despite numerous attempts the capital was still not forthcoming.

Matters soon took a remarkable turn. Various American businesses had been establishing themselves in areas of British industry, consequent on their own domestic expansion losing impetus. One such businessman, heavily involved in the American tramway industry, became interested in the dormant CCE&HR and purchased the powers for the line on 1st October 1900. The man was Charles Tyson Yerkes, of Chicago, who claimed to have backing worth thirty million pounds and the vision to see how London could be transformed by the provision of frequent electric railway services between the suburbs and the centre of town – and the vision to see how such services could produce the necessary reward for his syndicate.

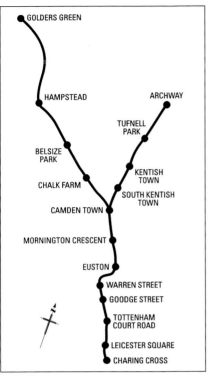

Left **The Charing Cross, Euston & Hampstead Railway as opened in 1907 (modern names used for ease of reference).**

But Yerkes did not stop at the CCE&HR. He took the opportunity to acquire a controlling interest in the Metropolitan District Railway, an ailing, steam operated sub-surface underground railway suffering badly from more modern competition. It was his intention to modernise and electrify the line to restore its fortunes. He also acquired control of a moribund but partly built tube – the Baker Street & Waterloo Railway (BS&WR) and the powers for two further tube schemes which he amalgamated into the Great Northern, Piccadilly & Brompton Railway (GNP&BR). Yerkes established a holding company on 15th July 1901 known as the Metropolitan District Electric Traction Company Limited; this was reconstituted on 9th April 1902 as the Underground Electric Railways Company of London Limited (UERL), providing greater capital opportunities (the UERL continued to operate much of London's transport until 1933).

In 1902 the specification of the line called for 11ft 6ins diameter running tunnels and not less than 21ft diameter station tunnels of 250ft length, equipped with wooden platforms and finished with tiles or enamelled bricks. Surface buildings were to be not more than one storey, and finishes and decorations were to be "fully equal to those of the best stations on the Central London Railway", and capable of carrying three additional storeys for later commercial use. Signalling was to permit of a five-minute interval service for which 25 motor cars and 75 trailers were deemed sufficient. The carriages were to be 'at least equal in quality to the carriages put on the New York elevated railway in 1892' and were to seat 48 passengers.

Work on tunnelling the CCE&HR started in September 1903 – after yet further changes had been sanctioned by Parliament on 18th November 1902. This authorised what was to the British mind a novel extension beyond Hampstead to the largely uninhabited pastures of Golders Green, achieved in the face of much opposition by those who thought the line would ruin the Heath; but it must be recalled that the line was now in the hands of Americans for whom such a speculative approach was thought usual. It had another benefit of considerably easing the gradients between Chalk Farm and Hampstead and offering comparatively cheap land at Golders Green for the depot and power station – a site in Hampstead had been authorised in the original Act. Further provisions permitted the Kentish Town branch to be extended northwards to a point near the Highgate station of the Great Northern Railway via an intermediate station at the bottom of Highgate Hill – this latter station, now called Archway, opened as Highgate and the portion, beyond, to Highgate (GNR) was not proceeded with.

The UERL acted as the main contractor for all three subsidiary tube companies, as a result of which common standards and a common style were adopted so far as possible. One of the most interesting features of the method of construction is that it was entirely in the hands of a team of American specialists, hand-picked for their expertise by Yerkes and accompanying him from the USA; much of the UERL's ideas were thus based on then current American practice (when their task was complete most of the team returned to the USA, although Yerkes himself did not live to see any of the tube schemes open). It was a bone of contention at the time that so much of the equipment used on the railway also came from the USA, despite earlier assurances to the contrary. For example, the steel rails were shipped across the Atlantic. The rolling stock was also American and it was said at the time that the delivery period for similar British built stock was too long – not, perhaps, an unfamiliar sentiment today!

Subcontractors for the CCE&HR tunnelling were Price & Reeves and the company made use of a Price rotary excavator – a power-driven excavator associated with a tunnelling shield – which was capable of driving 96 rings (160 feet) a week. Greathead shields were used in difficult areas. Tunnelling work was completed in December 1905 and activities turned towards equipping the line.

A station which had proved a special problem was Charing Cross, the terminus. The station lay beneath the South Eastern Railway station, which latter company objected to any work liable to interfere with road traffic access to its forecourt; as a result the CCE&HR were forced to contemplate constructing their lift shafts from the bottom upwards, to the level of the booking hall beneath the forecourt. However, in December 1905 the arched roof of the main line station collapsed and the station was closed for over three months while repair work was carried out. An agreement was quickly reached between the two companies and in the remarkably short time of six weeks the forecourt surface was excavated, the side walls of the booking hall were built and roofed over with girders and one of the lift shafts was excavated to its full depth – the remaining shaft being dug later from the covered booking hall.

By the time the railway had been completed some significant changes had been made to the specification and more cars had been ordered. The internal diameter of the running tunnels had been increased to 11ft 8¼ins. The platform tunnels were built 350ft long (enough for seven cars – to use the American parlance – not the five cars length originally specified), and the platforms were paved instead of being wooden, to improve fire protection. Three new stations had appeared, at Mornington Crescent (at the original Seymour Street site), Castle Road (between Kentish Town and Camden Town) and North End (between Hampstead and Golders Green), though at the latter the work was abandoned with only the platform tunnels complete, and it was never opened. Station tunnels were built to an internal diameter of 21ft 2½ins.

The construction of the cars was largely in steel and the internal finish comprised non-flammable mahogany. The electrical equipment was constructed by the British Thomson-Houston Company to American (GEC) specifications and was based on the multiple-unit system of control devised by Sprague, which had proved very successful on the Central London Railway. The two traction motors on the motor cars were each rated at 200hp. The braking system consisted of the well-established Westinghouse air brake. The 150 cars were built by the American Car & Foundry Company in the USA and shipped over and assembled in Manchester and brought down by rail; they were finally delivered to Golders Green by road. There were three types of car: 60 of the cars were motor cars, provided with a driving cab, single motor-bogie and an equipment compartment mounted over the motor-bogie. The remaining cars were

A view of the track outside Golders Green station, looking towards the tunnel mouth, prior to opening. In this open section signalling is by pneumatically controlled lower quadrant semaphore signals. LT Museum

unpowered: 50 (known as control trailers) had a driving position and the remaining 40 (known as trailers) did not. They were all painted a rich maroon colour described as Midland Lake and carried the initials of the company and fleet number in blocked gold lettering.

Power was not to be generated locally as arrangements were made for one main generating station at Lots Road, Chelsea, which was to provide electricity to the District Railway and all three UERL tube lines. The southern end of the CCE&HR was fed directly from the nearby District Railway substation at Charing Cross, and additional substations were built at Euston, Belsize Park, Golders Green and Kentish Town. In each of these four a pair of rotary converters was installed to convert the 11,000 volts, three phase ac supply to 550 volts dc for feeding the conductor rails and lifts.

Signalling was, where possible, completely automatic and operated by means of electrical track circuits which detected the presence of trains. The signals consisted of an electro-pneumatically controlled spectacle plate containing red and green coloured glasses which passed in front of a fixed oil (later electric) lamp – the coloured aspect shown indicated the presence or absence of a train ahead. In addition, an air-operated 'trainstop' lever afforded protection against a train passing a signal at danger. The trainstop's lever arm was inclined upwards by a spring when the signal showed red and would engage with a lever on a passing train to apply the emergency brakes. When a signal showed green the trainstop lever was depressed clear of the passage of trains by a compressed air motor. This system, though modernised, was for many years universal on the Underground.

Signal cabins were provided at Charing Cross, Mornington Crescent, Camden Town, Highgate, Hampstead and Golders Green owing to the presence of pointwork and crossovers. Westinghouse electro-pneumatic lever frames were installed with miniature levers to control points and associated signals. At Golders Green, in the open air, pneumatically controlled lower quadrant semaphore signals were erected.

Golders Green station forecourt. A connecting bus service (contracted to Birch Brothers) ran to the Bell Inn, Hendon. The tree growing through the canopy was encased when the sheltered area was extended and it remained in this form for some years.

Golders Green station and depot, although in the open country initially, were designed for handling extensive traffic should the opportunity arise. Hence the provision of four platform faces – the centre pair for departure and the outer faces for arrivals.

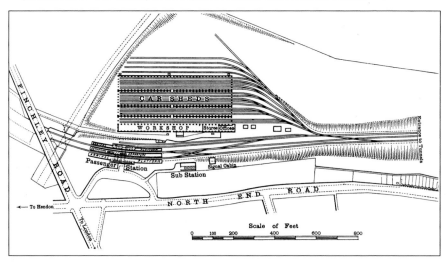

The 1907 ACF 'gate' stock was the first multiple unit stock on the Northern Line. Operated as five-car trains in busy periods, the sets were uncoupled to allow two-car sets to operate at quiet times. The leather strap-hangers suggest that, unlike the C&SLR, the CCE&HR was prepared for rush hour traffic from the outset. LT Museum

Stations were built to an essentially standard design, being steel-framed and clad in a ruby-red glazed tilework. They were of two storeys, with the upper floor used for the electric lift machinery and staff accommodation. Platform finishes had tiled walls, all to a similar characteristic theme but each adopting its own distinctive coloured pattern – said to be another American idea building on a theme used in New York. At Oxford Street and Charing Cross there were no station buildings and the booking hall was built beneath the street and main line station forecourt respectively. Interchange was provided at Leicester Square and Oxford Street with east-west tube lines, and at Euston with the City & South London (although a separate surface Charing Cross, Euston & Hampstead Railway station was built, there was also access to the ticket hall beneath the main line station, shared with the C&SLR).

The new railway opened for public traffic on 22nd June 1907, a Saturday, although still not quite complete in all details and thus remaining in the hands of the contractors for some weeks more. David Lloyd George, then President of the Board of Trade, opened the railway and tried his hand at driving a train using an engraved golden key with which he was subsequently presented. Amid a blaze of publicity the railway then opened its gates free to the public for the rest of the day. It was estimated that between 120 and 150 thousand passengers made use of this offer.

Interestingly, the Hampstead tube was the first to embody a tube junction and branches. This immediately created a need for passengers south of Camden Town to know where the northward-bound trains were going. Since the carriages were gate-ended there were plenty of staff to call the information out, but the trains also carried destination signs on the leading car. A system of coloured lights was also used. To warn the signalman at Camden Town of the correct destination of trains, plungers were installed at Mornington Crescent which northbound drivers had to operate.

Trains ran from Charing Cross to both Hampstead and Highgate, as the station at Archway was at first called; around a third of the Hampstead trains were projected to Golders Green where evidence of housing had already begun to appear. Trains were initially of five cars but three cars were stabled at quiet times leaving a two-car portion

Mornington Crescent was entirely typical of Leslie Green's exterior design of all stations on the CCE&HR except Golders Green. Where the design allowed, as in this case, the lifts deposited passengers directly into the street, and on corner sites the entrance was usually in a different face of the building. Lift equipment was housed in the upper floor.

(motor and control trailer) in service. Little changed for the first few years except some station renaming (Euston Road became Warren Street, Tottenham Court Road became Goodge Street, and Oxford Street became Tottenham Court Road).

Yerkes had always wanted his three tube lines to be operated as a single entity. This had proved troublesome in practice as each of them were separately constituted legal entities with their own powers, duties and obligations. It took until 1910 to gain parliamentary sanction for an adequate solution to the matter. This involved the absorption of the CCE&HR (and the Baker Street & Waterloo Railway) by the Great Northern Piccadilly & Brompton Railway which was renamed the London Electric Railway. The CCE&HR thenceforth became known as the LER's 'Hampstead' line. This allowed common ticketing and pooling of resources and receipts to be put on a proper footing, but for physical reasons there could be no interworking of trains.

The first extension was a projection of the line southwards from Charing Cross (which became 'Strand' station) to the District Line's station at Charing Cross. Although this was rather less than a quarter mile away the considerably improved interchange was felt to be worthwhile. The extension opened in 1914 in the form of a single track reversing loop, thus only one new platform was needed. The platform was sharply curved (being a part of the loop) and exists today as the northbound platform at what is now Embankment station.

The provision of a reversing loop introduced a problem which has remained with the line and its successors ever since. The carriages were delivered with the electrical inter-car jumpers and air hoses arranged on the assumption that the cars would never be turned round (which would put the jumpers on the wrong side). The loop meant that trains were frequently running 'wrong way round', thereby rendering them unable to couple properly with unturned stock. A minor problem, it may be thought, but one where the existence of cars which could not easily couple to others created a maintenance problem (more spares were needed) as well as operating difficulties in an emergency. In later years a turntable had to be installed at Golders Green in an attempt to ease the difficulty.

Highgate station around the time of the line's opening, showing general decor. Each station had platforms with a distinctive wall tile pattern, and colour schemes also varied. The signal box in the booth at the platform end and an overhead 'maxim' arc light are visible.

The Northern Line Emerges

Even while the CCE&HR was still on the drawing board there were plans for another venture, the Edgware and Hampstead Railway, which was intended to connect with the CCE&HR 'end on' at Hampstead; this pre-dated the CCE&HR's own Golders Green extension and would have provided a through route to Edgware. Negotiations between the two companies resulted in the UERL agreeing to take a controlling interest in the E&HR, and the route of the latter being modified to make an end-on connection at Golders Green (the E&HR's Hampstead section being abandoned). The authorising legislation received the Royal Assent in 1902, and although it had powers to operate as a (comparatively cheap) light railway, finance could still not be raised and little work was done. Nevertheless, when the CCE&HR opened, the tracks at Golders Green terminated on what was quite clearly a bridge abutment, poised for onward projection along the E&HR route. A further proposal for a Watford & Edgware Railway was also authorised, but although some land was purchased no work was done.

An early move following the formation of the LER was its formal absorption of the Edgware & Hampstead company and the urgent development of proposals to begin construction work in 1912; the railway had become in effect a northward extension of the Hampstead line through mainly unspoilt countryside to Edgware, considerable housing development – and new revenue – being anticipated. By this time the route between Golders Green and Hendon had been modified, a better route northwards through rapidly developing Golders Green being deemed necessary (unfortunately requiring demolition of some of the houses the railway had just encouraged to be built).

Summer 1923, and the station platform at Hendon begins to take shape amidst the fields.
LT Museum

A Fred Taylor poster illustrating, with some artistic licence, housebuilding around the newly-completed Brent station, opened in 1923. LT Museum

Although land acquisition had started, the First World War effectively put a stop to things. Afterwards it was amongst the Underground's more important priorities and with government support through the Trade Facilities Act – a general Act designed to promote employment – work proceeded immediately. Major contracts were placed in 1922 and progress was rapid with the extension opened as far as Hendon on 19th November 1923 and beyond to Edgware on 18th August 1924.

Stations were provided at Brent (now Brent Cross), Hendon Central, Colindale, Burnt Oak and Edgware. From Golders Green to Brent the line was largely on brick viaduct, with one deep cutting, although with the exception of a cutting and a section of tunnel near Hendon there was little in the way of extensive earthworks on the remainder of the line; the tunnels north of Hendon were standard twin tube tunnels of 11ft 8¼ins. A reversing siding was located between the running lines just north of Colindale. Signalling was automatic, and coloured light signals were installed for the first time in the open-air on the Underground. Signal cabins were required at Edgware, Colindale and Hendon. Provision was made at Brent for passing loops for 'non-stop' trains to overtake those in the platform. The loops and associated signal box were not commissioned until 1927 although the innovation was not long lived and they were taken out of use in 1936. A car shed and sidings for additional rolling stock were provided at Edgware, where a third platform was added in 1932.

Built on what was then the edge of Edgware village, Edgware station was planned as a railhead, with integrated bus feeder services biting deep into the catchment areas of the neighbouring Metropolitan, LNE and LM&S railways. LT Museum

Station buildings were spacious and were predominantly of neo-Georgian style faced with Portland stone. Edgware was of the Italianate school and was set back from the road to provide for a forecourt flanked by a pair of colonnades; this allowed for the feeder bus services, very necessary in the light of the thin population nearby. Burnt Oak was a more modest brick building reflecting the absence of promising traffic objectives at that time – even so, the station opened late, on 27th October 1924, owing to a builders' strike. A larger permanent building was opened in August 1928 when development in the area became extensive. At platform level a single 'island' arrangement was provided at all stations, with awnings for about a third of the length.

Considerable alterations were made at Golders Green where the entire track layout was remodelled and an additional platform face provided to allow trains reversing there to conflict as little as possible with the new through services. The substation was enlarged to share the supply to the extension with a new substation at Burnt Oak, which was remotely controlled from Golders Green. A further substation was opened at Hendon in 1930. The supply was taken from Lots Road generating station which had gradually been enlarged, although a few years later the Edgware extension was fed from a bulk supply provided by the Metropolitan Railway at Neasden.

In 1913 the City & South London Railway had been purchased by the UERL and had been integrated with the rest of the Underground, so far as possible. But there was no question of full integration while the C&SLR still operated its existing equipment and rolling stock, which was antiquated by prevailing standards (though none of it was more than 23 years old – such had been the rate of progress elsewhere). Various schemes were looked at, the major problem being the short platforms and restrictive diameter of the tunnels – only 10ft 2ins ruling diameter. It was rapidly decided that platform extension and tunnel enlargement would be the only answer, and this would be coupled with a link with the Hampstead line at Camden Town which would make use of the capacity available on the northern branches and provide a through route to the City.

Although the necessary powers were obtained in 1913 it was not possible to proceed at once, and the war stopped any idea of immediate activity: but deferral did not prevent some equipment modernisation. Stockwell power station was closed in 1915 and high tension ac power was taken from comparatively efficient Lots Road; Hopkinson's 5-wire dc distribution system was abandoned and new substations were installed at Stockwell, Elephant & Castle and Old Street, with a dc feed taken from the Hampstead substation at Euston which was enlarged. Angel and London Bridge booster stations were closed at the same time. From 1919 the existing mechanical signalling equipment was replaced by a fully track circuited ac electro-pneumatic system, similar to the UERL standard though without provision of trainstops – the locomotives were not fitted with tripcocks and 'assistant' drivers were still carried. The final section of new signalling, from Stockwell to Clapham Common, came into use on 1st January 1922.

Work on the extension from Euston to Camden Town also started in 1922, and to allow fast progress on tunnel enlargement the existing railway was closed between Moorgate Street and Euston from Wednesday 9th August that year. On the remainder of the line Borough (and later Kennington) closed to allow the platforms to be used as worksites as it was the intention to keep the railway in operation between Clapham Common and Moorgate Street while the reconstruction proceeded all around. For this purpose a shield was devised which allowed trains to pass exposed clay during the day at the worksites where the tunnels were being enlarged at night. To aid matters the railway was opened later in the morning and the evening service was curtailed, last trains leaving the termini at 7.14pm. An auxiliary bus service, run by the C&SLR, was operated along the portion of the line temporarily closed and stopped intermediately only at King's Cross, Angel, City Road and Old Street. From the start of 1923 this service was withdrawn and replaced by a new service operating along the whole of the line to relieve the inevitable congestion arising at all stations through reduced services.

Stockwell depot became the principal worksite and base for numerous works' trains. Spare stock and nine service trains were outstabled in the tunnel north of Moorgate Street to make more room, although some spare coaches were stabled in a siding laid along part of the disused King William Street branch. Initially a two-minute interval service of 5-coach trains was operated but this became troublesome in the face of increasing numbers of speed restrictions and (later) areas of single line working south of Oval. As the railway increasingly took on the appearance of a vast building site the service latterly dropped back to four-minute intervals. Towards the end of 1923 some 19,000 out of 22,000 tunnel rings had been enlarged, in many instances by re-using existing segments with additional key pieces inserted within each tunnel ring, and work was proceeding at some sixty sites.

During reconstruction at Borough and Kennington stations, temporary sidings for engineers' trains were installed on the former platform sites. LT Museum

At 5.12pm on 27th November 1923 railway traffic came to a dramatic halt. At a point near Borough, where the existence of a sand and gravel overlay was anticipated, special construction had just started to avoid disturbing the tunnel crown during enlargement. The tunnel crown had been temporarily removed but it was not realised that there was unsound ground only inches above the veneer of clay at this point. The railway might have carried on unscathed had not a protective board somehow become dislodged and hit by a passing train which disturbed the delicate status quo immediately above. The driver stopped the train and removed the wood from the line then the guard reported water and gravel coming into the tunnel near the rear. Fortunately the driver managed to extract the train and get it to Borough before the traction current went off. Within 15 minutes the tunnel was completely blocked by the inrush and in due course about 650 tons of gravel settled down to await removal. As a result of this subsidence a huge crater formed beneath Newington Causeway some forty feet above. Surprisingly the road surface remained undisturbed for about fifty minutes when a build up of gas beneath, where an unsupported gas main had failed, caused a huge explosion. The gaping hole thus uncovered remained alight from the ignition of escaping gas until an unsupported water main failed and put out the fire. Dramatically closed by force of circumstances the entire railway was not re-opened until reconstruction was completed. The bus service was somewhat strengthened during this period.

The first section of the C&SLR to re-open was the portion from Moorgate (the 'Street' was dropped) to Euston and the connection with the Hampstead line at Camden Town. Through trains from Moorgate to Hendon were run from the outset on 20th April 1924. City Road station was permanently closed as traffic there had been very light. South of Moorgate the line was re-opened on 1st December 1924. At Euston the lifts (joint with the Hampstead line) were retained as were those at King's Cross, Angel, Bank, London Bridge, Borough, Elephant & Castle and Kennington, which were all modernised.

At the remaining stations it was decided to replace the lifts with escalators although they were not completed (except at Stockwell) at the time of re-opening and the old lifts had to be retained temporarily. It should be noted in passing that electric lifts had replaced the hydraulic lifts at the original stations before the First World War. In most cases the new escalators led from existing station superstructures although at Moorgate a new ticket hall was built at basement level and at Clapham Common a new station site was selected with the ticket hall beneath the roadway. Borough and Kennington stations, which had been worksites, were also delayed in opening. All platforms were modernised, retiled and extended from 200 to 350 feet; at Stockwell the old single station tunnel was abandoned and replaced by twin platform tunnels immediately to the south.

At both Kennington and Elephant & Castle the positions of the northbound tracks and platforms were transposed to ease alignments, requiring some station remodelling (extensively so at Kennington). After clearing up operations the depot at Stockwell was closed and sold for housing, most of the locomotives were cut up and the rolling stock was disposed of.

Much of the signalling had already been modernised, but some further works were undertaken, partly to cater for physical changes. For example the sidings at Moorgate, Old Street, London Bridge and Elephant & Castle had been lost (the sidings at Angel, Stockwell and Euston survived until the 1950s and 1960s). The power supply system was altered to cater for the standard 4-rail arrangement with outside positive rail and centre negative. The junctions at Camden Town required extensive and complex construction work and when completed allowed trains from either route southwards to proceed to either route northwards, and vice versa, with minimal conflict. The network of tunnels was built around the existing junction with almost no disturbance to passenger services.

The much improved capacity of the C&SLR following reconstruction meant that extension could be contemplated southwards from Clapham Common into the open fields of Surrey, near Morden, via busy Balham and Tooting. Powers were obtained in 1923 and these also allowed for a link between Kennington and Charing Cross, thus offering a choice of central London destinations for those living south of the river. This would require high capacity junction work at Kennington only marginally less complicated than that which was about to come into service at Camden Town (see diagram opposite).

Work began in earnest on the Morden extension early in 1924, while that for the Kennington – Charing Cross link began in April the same year. Progress was rapid and both new lines were opened on 13th September 1926, though not all work was quite complete and Balham station opened only in December.

South of Strand station the new southbound line diverged from the loop to proceed through a new platform at Charing Cross – the northbound line diverged south of the existing platform, which was retained, explaining the sharp reverse curvature inherited today. Twin tubes continued through new platforms at Waterloo (where the existing Bakerloo Line station was enlarged to cope with the new line and provided with escalators). The tubes continued to Kennington where new platforms flanked the old City & South London station. Just to the south, running connections were made with the C&SLR while for a proportion of the Hampstead line's service a new reversing loop was constructed, preserving the complications loops presented to the rolling stock position. A new double length siding was also built there, principally for C&SLR trains to use, as they could not gain access to the loop.

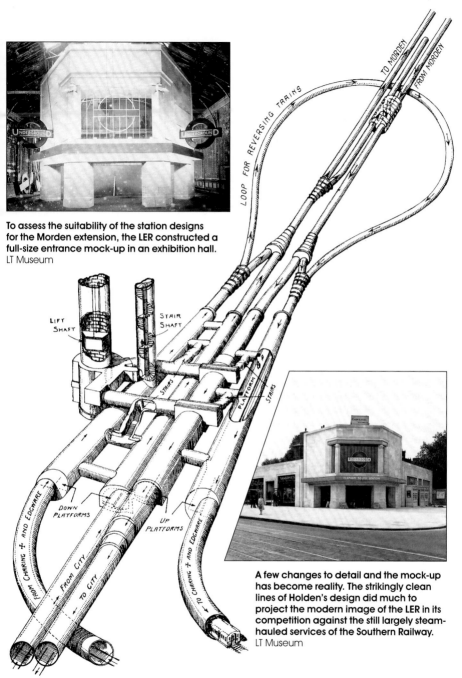

To assess the suitability of the station designs for the Morden extension, the LER constructed a full-size entrance mock-up in an exhibition hall.
LT Museum

A few changes to detail and the mock-up has become reality. The strikingly clean lines of Holden's design did much to project the modern image of the LER in its competition against the still largely steam-hauled services of the Southern Railway.
LT Museum

The reconstruction work at Kennington required the provision of a reversing loop and two new flanking platforms as well as the transposition of one of the running lines with an existing platform. A centre reversing siding (an afterthought) was also provided.
M.A.C.Horne Collection

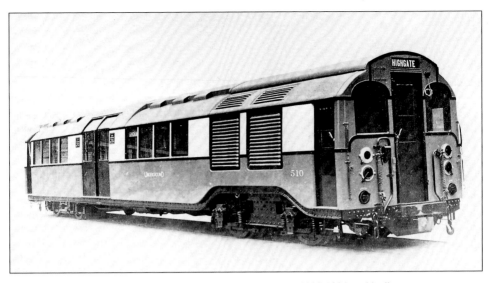

A car of the rolling stock purchased for the extensions of 1923-1926 and for the replacement of earlier stock. F. Moore

South of Clapham Common twin tubes ran most of the way to Morden and new stations were opened at Clapham South, Balham, Trinity Road (later renamed Tooting Bec), Tooting Broadway, South Wimbledon and Colliers Wood. Morden was built as an open air station with three tracks and five platforms. Beyond the station the line continued into a new depot, primarily arranged for stabling sidings with limited repair and maintenance facilities. The new stations were all built in a similar style, much influenced by the architectural fashion of Charles Holden and making considerable use of Portland stone facing. At the lower level, stations had individual platforms for each direction of travel and in all cases escalators came down to a concourse between them (in many cases the escalators carried people directly from platform to street level). The older, reconstructed C&SLR stations were modernised to look similar in style where possible – though adapting existing stations rarely produced an ideal result; for example tortuous passages were often necessary when shoehorning escalators in, especially when existing surface buildings were retained. South Kentish Town (as Castle Road was called upon opening) closed with effect from 18th August 1924.

To service the new extensions and to replace the antiquated C&SLR locomotives and carriages, a substantial order was placed for new rolling stock. Following some experimental cars delivered in 1922 orders were placed for successive batches of new cars of all-steel construction and fitted with air-operated doors (allowing a reduction in trainstaff to a driver and two guards per train – reduced to one guard in 1927). Most of this stock arrived between 1923 and 1926, numbering 181 motor cars, 100 trailers and 128 control trailers; ownership was divided between the LER and C&SLR, though this did not affect maintenance or operation of the cars. Later batches of similar stock also allowed the Hampstead line's old gate-ended cars to be scrapped (the last one ran on 31st January 1929) and train lengths to be standardised at 7-cars. When this had been achieved the stockholding for the combined lines was 724 cars.

Platforms on the Morden extension stations were similar in design, being clad in the then 'house style' of white and green glazed tiles. LT Museum

Poster proclaiming the achievement of the rebuilding of the City & South London Railway; the Northern Line as we now know it had substantially taken shape. LT Museum

FROM EUSTON TO CLAPHAM COMMON
THE TRANSFORMATION
IS COMPLETE

Within a few years a typical timetable requirement was for a 95 train peak service (of 665 cars) with trains every 1½-2 minutes via Charing Cross (more or less equally from Highgate and Edgware) and every 2-3 minutes via Bank, with a preponderance of trains from Edgware rather than Highgate. All the Bank and about a third of the Charing Cross trains ran to Morden. Some trains terminated short at Tooting, Golders Green or Colindale. During the midday off-peak a slightly less intensive service of short trains was run, 4-cars Edgware to Kennington via Charing Cross, 3-cars Golders Green to Morden via Bank, and 3-cars Highgate to Morden via Charing Cross. Some short trains also ran in the evenings.

Although both the LER and the C&SLR continued separate legal existences under the UERL umbrella, the conglomeration resulting from the new junctions and through services meant that the companies had no option but to function as a single operational railway. With a route from Morden to Kennington, thence two possible routes to Euston and Camden Town, and two northern branches (to Edgware or Highgate), it is clear that by 1926 the basis of the present day Northern Line already existed. In fact the name Northern Line was not coined until 1937, and in the meantime such less than satisfactory names as 'Hampstead & City Line' and 'Edgware–Morden Line' had to suffice.

The complex new services created an urgent need for equipment to describe for the passenger's benefit both the destination and routeing of the trains. This equipment already existed at signal cabins (the signalmen only rarely being able to see the trains) and the apparatus was extended to the majority of stations, information being displayed on platforms by means of illuminated glass signs, which were to have a life of over 60 years. Initially the new trains carried above the cab door a roller blind with the destinations on it, and beneath this was a swivelling plate showing the route. In later batches of stock the information was given by destination plates displayed below the offside cab window, the earlier cars being modified to suit.

To cope with the increased traffic resulting from the modernisation and extensions several central London stations had to be improved. At Tottenham Court Road the lifts were replaced by escalators. Three escalators were constructed from the old Hampstead Line ticket hall to a new intermediate concourse which connected with the Central London Railway platforms, the old CLR ticket hall being closed; two further escalators led from the intermediate concourse to the Hampstead Line platforms. All these were brought into use between September 1925 and February 1926. In April 1933 further relief was afforded by an additional escalator between the concourse to a point half way along the Hampstead Line platforms. At Leicester Square lifts were dispensed with in May 1935, a spacious and impressive new booking hall having been constructed beneath the road surface with a triple bank of escalators leading to a circulating area just above the Hampstead Line platform level, to which it was connected by stairs; further escalators led from the ticket hall to the Piccadilly Line. At Warren Street a new booking hall and escalators were provided in September 1933. Lifts were also dispensed with at Camden Town (October 1929), Highgate (June 1931) and Kentish Town (November 1932) where in each case a pair of escalators was installed, although the existing emergency spiral stairways were retained. At Bank escalators were installed from the south end of the Northern Line platforms to Monument station on the District Line, coming into service on 18th September 1933.

Opposite **Before the Second World War, air displays at RAF Hendon attracted huge crowds, most of whom chose to travel by the cheap and frequent tube services to Colindale. For many this was their first view of the north London suburbs.** LT Museum

A New Works Programme

The year 1933 saw the creation of London Transport. On 1st July all the underground railways, the buses and the trams were transferred to the new London Passenger Transport Board, to give the organisation its full title. Of course, many of the services had already been a part of the old UERL group (including most of the buses and a proportion of the trams) but it was hoped that the enforced co-ordination would bring greater efficiency and better services.

Even more relevant was the simultaneous establishment of the London Passenger Transport Pool. This was administered by a Standing Joint Committee consisting of the new LPTB and representatives of the main line railway companies. Within the LPTB area *all* revenue related to local passenger journeys was pooled, and shared out in agreed proportions. This meant that developments and service alterations made by any one of the constituents would have an effect on the revenues of them all, though to different degrees. In turn it meant that there was an enforced measure of co-operation needed between members of the pool, and the Standing Joint Committee (rather than the LPTB alone) emerged as the central planning authority for London's new services.

Even in 1933 and 1934 considerable planning work was being done in the expectation that money would be made available for a substantial scheme of expansion. There were several areas around the system where there was a clear demand for service improvement or extension of services. In the area north of Highgate Underground station the residents frequently registered their dissatisfaction with existing transport facilities and extensions had been contemplated on more than one occasion (though never commanding priority). There was, for example, a proposal to extend the Highgate branch to Muswell Hill as long previously as 1919. It is worth the reminder that 'Highgate' is now the station we call Archway (it was renamed Archway [Highgate] in 1939, with the suffix dropped two years later) and that there was considerable latent capacity available after 1924, the Highgate branch having only three stations north of Camden Town against the nine of the Edgware branch.

Another line which came under the microscope was the former Great Northern & City Railway which sported only six stations and ran between Moorgate and Finsbury Park – a tube railway (opened in 1904) but unusually built to main line gauge. Here, there was a large volume of awkward interchange at Finsbury Park from the main line and the buses and trams, yet the line itself had extra capacity available. Plans emerged for northward extension and through running onto the main line railway above.

What emerged after two years of rumours, debate and political manoeuvring was a massive scheme of improvements estimated to cost some £40 million. The money was to be raised by a statutory finance corporation at low interest and backed by a treasury guarantee. The work included replacement of trams by trolleybuses, some main line railway suburban electrification, Underground line modernisation, and projection of Underground trains over main line tracks, electrified for the purpose.

The effect on the Northern Line was a proposal to extend the Highgate branch northwards to East Finchley, thence to take over the existing London & North Eastern

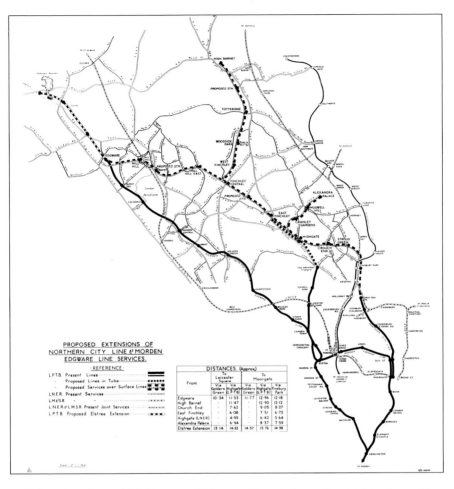

PROPOSED EXTENSIONS OF
NORTHERN CITY LINE & MORDEN
EDGWARE LINE SERVICES.

Railway branches to High Barnet and Edgware. The existing station at Highgate would be renamed Archway, and there would be an intermediate station beneath the existing Highgate (LNER) station, with which there would be interchange. An additional scheme emerged to link the Great Northern & City tube to a new line through Finsbury Park (LNER) station and thence take over the Alexandra Palace branch, but with through trains also to the High Barnet and Edgware branches. The whole network would then be operated as one railway.

The LNER branch between Finsbury Park and Edgware had opened in 1867, with the Finchley–High Barnet section following in 1872 and Highgate–Alexandra Palace in 1873. By the early 1930s there were 54 trains a day from High Barnet and 43 from the Alexandra Palace branch. Edgware to Church End (at Finchley) was generally worked as a shuttle service, but with a few through trains. The service from these branches worked to King's Cross, Moorgate or Broad Street and the journey time from Barnet to Moorgate was around 47 minutes (the present time for this journey is 38 minutes and there are over 130 trains to London destinations from Barnet alone).

41

The necessary powers for the Northern Line extensions were obtained in 1935 and 1936. Work on the link between Archway and East Finchley began in November 1936. This involved converting the northbound siding into the beginning of the new running tunnel while adapting the other one into what would be a centre reversing siding. At the East Finchley end the new tube tunnels would emerge either side of the existing LNER line and then proceed into the station, which required complete rebuilding.

To make life even more interesting, it was realised that the existing depot accommodation would be inadequate for these much expanded services and consideration was given to an extension north of Edgware over the proposed Watford & Edgware Railway alignment to Aldenham, where a large new depot would be erected. The area was almost entirely in open country and again there was a hope that speculative development would justify such an extension. The scheme required the complete rebuilding of Edgware station to allow for through running either from the Golders Green direction or from Finchley, there being a link planned from the nearby LNER branch which was being electrified.

Work on the Edgware reconstruction began in 1937 and eventually resulted in complete revision of the stabling siding layout and the demolition of the bus garage and the east wing of the station to allow for doubling the width of the station cutting. The station was to be rebuilt to allow large scale bus-rail interchange. The LNER line north of Finsbury Park was to be electrified and resignalled to Underground standards, most of which work was begun and continued while trains were running. Between Finchley Central and Edgware, however, the line was single track and had to be doubled. To allow this work to proceed quickly the service between these two points was suspended from 10th September 1939 and a temporary bus service substituted (this had operated previously during the midday period and on Sundays).

Bushey Heath station, at the junction of Elstree Road and the Watford By-Pass, was to be the focal point of a new shopping centre with a cinema and pub opposite, and subways leading from the station underneath both roads. The station design bore a considerable resemblance to Cockfosters Piccadilly Line station.

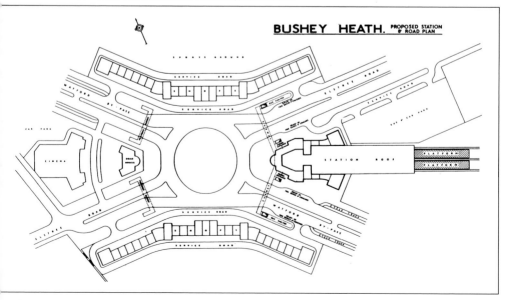

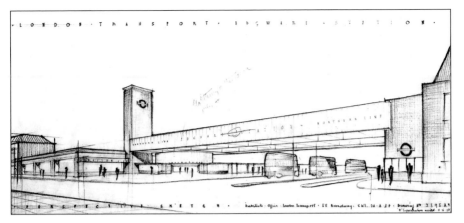

Access and interchange were planned for all the new and modified stations. Edgware's successful bus feeder services were to be catered for by building a new covered bus station alongside, with an enlarged bus garage behind the station. A characteristic brick tower would emphasise the LPTB station presence with a highly visible roundel sign. At Mill Hill (The Hale) a new combined station building serving both LPTB and LM&SR stations would provide covered interchange, whilst a rebuilt forecourt proposed new shop units with improved foot and road access.

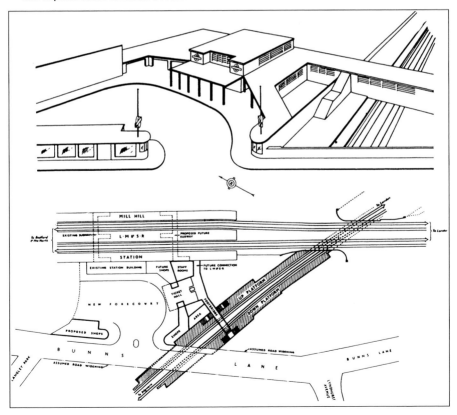

At Edgware reconstruction envisaged most of the trains from Bushey Heath running via Finchley Central, with services from both branches also terminating at Edgware. This post-war photo of Edgware shows the enlarged station and unused additional platforms. Photomatic

Facing page Arches constructed opposite the junction of Spur Road and the A41 at Edgware, the site of the planned Brockley Hill station. Bushey Heath depot was to have become the main depot on the Northern Line, replacing the cramped facilities at Golders Green. The main depot buildings were constructed and equipped in advance of the trackwork, lest they be required for essential war work in the looming conflict, which they were. In this post-war view a hut has been added (left foreground) which partly obscures the lifting shop (extreme left). Photomatic/LT Museum

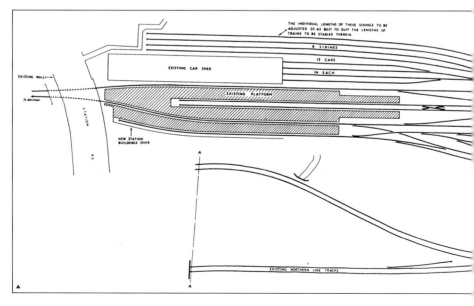

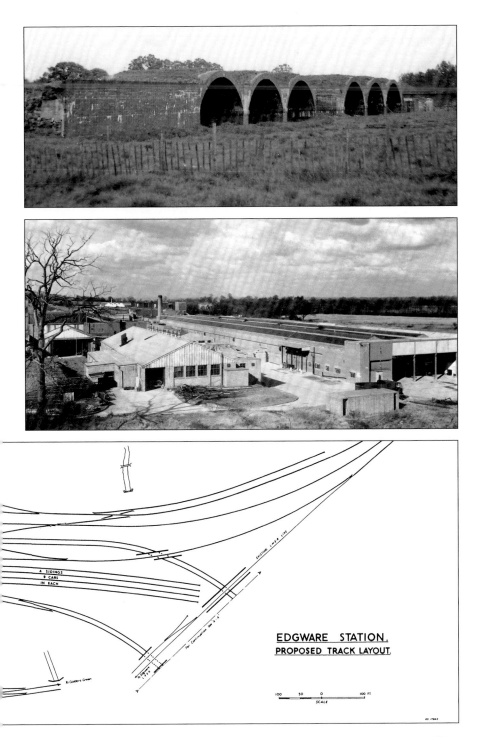

EDGWARE STATION,
PROPOSED TRACK LAYOUT.

4 SIDINGS
9 CARS
IN EACH

100   50   0   100 FT.
SCALE

With the extension of the Northern Line to East Finchley, the original GNR station building dating from the 1860s was demolished and a new building to the design of Adams, Holden and Pearson was constructed. By the northern bridge abutment a 10ft-high statue of an archer was erected, now the house symbol of the Northern Line. LT Museum

Early plans considered the possibility of building additional stations between Totteridge and High Barnet, between East Finchley and Church End (which became Finchley Central) and between Mill Hill East and Mill Hill (the Hale). None of these were pursued at the time and subsequent events have failed to indicate any current need. Elsewhere it was intended to provide entirely reconstructed stations at East Finchley, Finchley Central (which would gain a fourth platform), Mill Hill (the Hale), Edgware and High Barnet. The East Finchley station was completed almost in entirety and sported a large sculpture in the form of an archer. Only minor work was undertaken at Finchley Central – including part of the new platform – and for reasons to be given shortly little other work was done, existing stations having to suffice.

At Drayton Park work began on constructing ramps up to surface level and the whole of the GN&CR was modernised with the standard current rail system and modern signalling. This required replacing the existing type of sub-surface rolling stock with standard tube stock. The extension between Archway and East Finchley opened on 3rd July 1939, although the intermediate Highgate station was not ready until January 1941.

Scenes at East Finchley two weeks before the Northern Line arrived. LNER steam passes the newly built signal box, while a large banner straddles the Great North Road to announce the impending introduction of Underground services. J.Bonell

Edgware station, LNER, which closed to passengers in April 1940. A Sainsbury's supermarket occupies most of this land today.

The combined station at Highgate had four entrances: the entrance from Archway Road by the 'Woodman' public house was to have a pair of escalators to traverse the sixty or so feet from pavement to platform. In the event this part of the scheme was deferred and it was not until August 1957 that a single up escalator was put into service. M.A.C.Horne

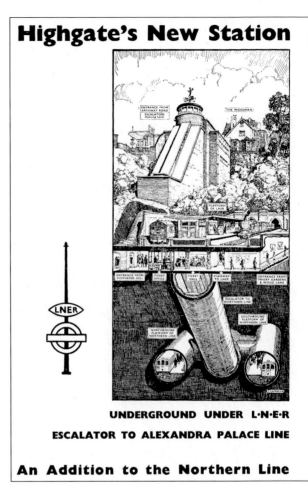

Highgate's New Station

UNDERGROUND UNDER L·N·E·R

ESCALATOR TO ALEXANDRA PALACE LINE

An Addition to the Northern Line

To operate the Northern Line extensions additional rolling stock was necessary. It was eventually decided to provide the Northern Line entirely with new high capacity trains, and transfer the existing trains to other lines. The new stock was smart and had semi-streamlined cabs; the main development introduced on these trains was the fact of the compressors and motor control equipment being mounted underfloor which, together with more compact motors, allowed the whole of the car's interior to be utilised for passengers (on the motor cars of all earlier stocks the equipment was mounted in a compartment behind the driver). The practical effect of this was that a 7-car train of the new type had the same carrying capacity as an 8-car train of the old.

Unlike earlier trains the cars were permanently coupled into 3-car or 4-car units, with automatic couplers at the ends of each unit to enable longer trains to be formed. There were no control trailers in this arrangement, as all end cars were motor cars with driving cabs. In the 4-car units there was a new kind of car called a non-driving motor car, which looked like a trailer but had motors fitted. Thus in any 7-car train five cars would be motored, giving a faster rate of acceleration and better adhesion than on the old stock. The new trains (1121 cars) became known as the 1938 stock, and the Northern Line was completely re-equipped between June 1938 and 1940, the older cars being transferred to the Central Line. Some of the 1938 stock was also operated on the Bakerloo Line.

The concept of 9-car trains was one of several ideas tried in an attempt to further increase the capacity of the Northern Line. Following experimental work, a single 9-car train was introduced from November 1937 and from February 1938 several trains were operated on the West End branch where they became a regular feature. Platform lengths were increased by an appropriate amount on the open-air stations between Golders Green and Edgware, but only minor changes could be made at tunnel stations where the restricted platform lengths meant that two cars would always be outside the platform. The mode of operation was that advance warning was given to passengers that the rear two cars would stop in the tunnel between Hampstead and Kennington southbound, except at Tottenham Court Road where these cars would then empty (giving passengers for that station a more comfortable journey). Northbound, the front cars were isolated between Kennington and Leicester Square, the rear cars being cut out between Tottenham Court Road and Golders Green, providing comfort to Leicester Square passengers and empty seats for Tottenham Court Road boarders. For the guard to be able to keep a look-out at all stations he had to ride on the seventh car which was provided with various controls and door cut-out switches to ensure that only doors in the platform opened. There were thoughts of substantial numbers of 9-car trains being introduced to service the new extensions, and extensive provision for them was proposed in terms of platform and siding lengths. In the event only ten 1938 stock trains were planned as 9-car trains, and wartime conditions put paid to this idiosyncratic mode of operation with only the first two having entered service. The cars were later modified for normal operation.

The 1938 Stock benefited from developments in mechanical design which allowed much control equipment to be located beneath seats and under the floor. Consequently the interior was uncluttered and provided more seats and far greater standing area than the cars which it replaced. LT Museum

The Northern Line at War

War came a little early to the Northern Line. Air raids had become a feature of the latter part of the first world war, and Blitzkrieg tactics had been well demonstrated during the Spanish Civil War. Two years later, in the autumn of 1938, came the threat of German expansion: when this culminated in the Munich Crisis talks Britain was alive to the threat of imminent bombing. It was recognised that London would be in the forefront of the attacks; also that the Underground network was under threat from flooding through bombed water mains or penetration of the cross-Thames tubes. Given this threat, and fearing the flooding of the entire central London network, it was therefore understandable that drastic measures should be taken.

During the evening of 27th September 1938 services were withdrawn between Strand (now Charing Cross) and Kennington, and over the following hours the tunnels were plugged with concrete to seal them against flooding. This particular disruption, though serious, was fairly short-lived. Neville Chamberlain had soon returned with a promise of "Peace in our time", and the crisis was over. The concrete was broken out and the West End branch lived again on 8th October. It had been, of course, a grim foretaste of what was to follow.

Less than two months after the Northern Line's forward looking extension to East Finchley, with more promised soon, the inevitable onset of war became closer: on 1st September 1939, carefully prepared plans to evacuate children got underway. To reduce congestion at main line termini, plans included the use of the Underground to carry children to outer suburban railheads, where fleets of buses carried them to the main line. Thus train-loads of youngsters – some eager to start a new life, but others in tears – were carried out to Edgware and thence by bus to New Barnet and the North. On the same day the link between Strand and Kennington was again lost, the tunnels plugged once more and work started on installing floodgates so that services could continue away from the Thames during raids (it would otherwise have been necessary to close the entire central area network). War was, of course, declared on 3rd September with an immediate reduction in optional traffic: people stayed at home; for a few weeks at least all theatres and cinemas closed. Art galleries and some offices had also left for the duration.

Although the cross-Thames tunnels on the City Branch were significantly deeper than those to the west, it was quickly realised that these also presented a risk of breach and on 7th September they too were plugged. Services from the north thus terminated at Moorgate and Strand, trains from Morden terminated no further north than London Bridge: the Northern was cut in two. This caused extensive congestion on parallel bus and tram routes.

It was also necessary to close a number of stations which were regarded as 'low lying' and in danger of flooding the system in the event of water mains being hit. Seven of these were on the Northern: Tooting Broadway, Tooting Bec (then Trinity Road), Balham, Clapham Common, Old Street, King's Cross and Tottenham Court Road. In all cases street access was blocked by concrete plugs but interchange between lines was

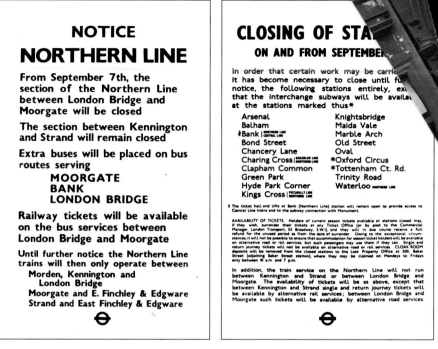

Posters announcing the closure of stations near the Thames or close to water mains so that tunnels or escalator shafts in danger of flooding by bomb damage could be plugged.

still possible at the last three (a situation which would not be allowed by today's safety considerations).

The blackout was also a problem – gallons of white paint were used on obstructions at open stations as a substitute for lighting but this did nothing to help identification of the hapless passenger's destination. Windows were by this time covered with anti-blast netting which rendered identification of surroundings quite impossible after dark. The driver's lookout window did not, of course, have netting but even so station staff had to provide a hurricane lamp by the stopping mark at each platform to assist drivers. The drivers themselves were also under instruction to coast as much as possible – to save energy – but also particularly over current rail gaps to minimise the risk of arcing which is highly visible from the air after dark.

The early months of the war had proved to be something of an anti-climax. There was a little time to provide refinements here and there: for example, passengers on trains were provided with dim blue lighting and reading lights for use in the open sections, although the latter were extinguished during raids. Everyone was asked to dig for victory – many trackside stretches were converted to allotments by staff and neighbours, and many proved quite long lasting. Some in the vicinity of Whetstone and High Barnet were still going strong until considerations of safety and the 'weed-killing' train finally extinguished them in the mid-1980s. Land in Underground ownership for the extensions was cultivated for canteen produce and the horses used there were fed on hay from around the system on embankments.

Blast shelters were erected outside all stations – as here at Goodge Street – to minimise the effect of a bomb exploding nearby. Like all pavement obstructions the blast shelters were edged with white paint to be distinguishable in black-out conditions. LT Museum

Special shelter arrangements were made by many authorities for those children not evacuated from London. On the platform wall can be seen the bunk position numbers, duplicated on shelter tickets. The posters give general guidance and instructions to adult shelterers. LT Museum

Although the Underground was officially a 'protected industry', avoiding major loss of labour to the armed forces, many employees did enter the King's service and it was necessary, as in the First World War, to bring women into uniformed jobs then regarded as the property of men. The first started work in September 1940: after the war the numbers of women declined and it was not until the late 1970s that any significant headway was made again to bring women into the industry.

The quieter period in the early months had seen the progressive provision of floodgates in stations and tunnels, allowing through services to be resumed on the Charing Cross branch on 17th December 1939, and through the City on 19th May 1940. The new gates restricted platform lengths, however, and special instructions were issued to guards concerning train door operation at Waterloo and London Bridge.

Continuing work on the extensions had allowed the Northern Line to replace LNER steam passenger services to High Barnet on 14th April 1940. From this date the London Transport fare-scale applied, though the line remained in main line ownership. At the same time the ticket office at the LNER station at Edgware was closed to passengers and its business was transferred to the Underground station a few hundred yards away – in practice this simply involved moving the ticket stock and the turning point for the railway replacement bus service.

The new Highgate station was opened in an incomplete state on 19th January 1941. A pair of platforms flanked escalators to a new ticket hall built beneath the LNER platforms, to which it was linked by stairs (the old LNER ticket office being closed). Street access was provided to Priory Gardens and somewhat more lengthy approaches from the Archway Road; works on the top flight of escalators and an entrance by the 'Woodman' were suspended.

There was a final extension from Finchley Central to Mill Hill East on 18th May 1941 to serve the Inglis Barracks (the replacement bus shuttle was cut back to run from Edgware to Mill Hill East at the same time). The remaining extension works had been abandoned in June 1940 "for the duration" although the new trains continued to arrive until 1941. The electrification of the Alexandra Palace branch also came to grief, despite the work already completed, although the branch did enter the London Transport fares system. Initially the steam train services from Finsbury Park continued to operate both to Alexandra Palace and to East Finchley (offering cross-platform interchange with electric services northwards). The East Finchley steam service was withdrawn from 3rd March 1941 (requiring rather less convenient interchange at Highgate), while the Alexandra Palace service gradually degenerated.

Work on the section north of Edgware had only begun fairly late in 1939 and took the form of earthworks, construction of twin-tube tunnels and depot buildings at Aldenham. When this work, too, stopped late in 1940 there was little to show, though the partly built tunnels were appreciated by the military who adapted them as a firing range. The depot buildings were pushed forward in an adapted form and became part of an aircraft factory as part of a scheme to construct Halifax bombers.

The war also required staff procedures to be developed in new ways. Early in 1940 staff were instructed on the handling of the various categories of raid alert (not all of which were declared publicly) and provision was made for the control function to move during raids from Leicester Square to underground locations at Camden Town and Kennington for the northern and southern sections of the line respectively. As thoughts returned to the more dire considerations of invasion it was recognised that the Underground offered excellent opportunities for enemy troop movements, which were to be prevented by the simple expedient of discharging traction current.

During the raids in 1917 residents had taken to the Underground to shelter. This time round the government feared that a 'deep shelter mentality' would develop, with people refusing to come out. At the outset of the war the use of Underground stations as shelters was therefore banned. This caused few problems during the 'phoney war' period but once the enemy's attention was turned towards Britain in 1940 circumstances changed dramatically. Air raids started in August of that year and by the following month, whatever the wishes of the authorities, Underground stations were *de facto* deep level shelters.

The government soon acknowledged reality and recognised that the demand for a quiet night amongst the inner-city dwellers could not be ignored (it was also realised that fears of people refusing to leave after raids were actually ill-founded). It was also later noticeable that the platforms were becoming rather smelly, and by October provisions were in hand for improved sanitation and for bunks. Demand was high; tickets were issued and it was decided to open both the disused stations at South Kentish Town and City Road, and the unfinished station at Highgate. Special trains were run to convey shelterers to and from these locations and later on specials were run to carry refreshments too.

The shelterers came to be quite at home on the tube over the twelve months from August 1940: some were even born there. The presence of these refugees from the surface did not help the passage of those still on their way home to the more distant suburbs though – thousands of passengers had to pick their way over slumbering bodies and sometimes by mid-evening stations were closed to avoid danger from congestion. Borough station, for example, was closed at 9 o'clock in the evening on 12th September 1940 "owing to enormous congestion of people taking shelter from air raids". The disused C&SLR tunnels from Borough to King William Street were also converted for use as local authority air raid shelters.

The start of the blitz in August 1940 brought problems peculiar to the Northern, in that with each raid the cross-Thames sections were closed down, dividing the line into two. The low-lying stations were also closed and made watertight. This action certainly saved the day at Tooting Broadway on 7th October 1940, when a 30 inch (760 mm) water main was destroyed just outside the station. On the other hand, with a relatively low proportion of its route in the open air, the Northern managed to escape some of the lengthy disruption experienced on the surface.

There were, regrettably, two major incidents affecting the line – one at Bank in January 1941 when the subway system serving the Central Line ticket hall suffered a direct hit; the other, more seriously for the Northern when a bomb breached the tunnels at Balham station, filling the platforms and tunnels to within 100 yards of Clapham South with soil, water and gas from shattered mains.

In some ways more disruptive, though, were the persistent closures and instances of damage from more minor incidents which affected service, staff and passengers on a daily basis for a year. Unexploded bombs sometimes caused service suspensions – two weeks in one case, between Golders Green and Colindale because of the threat from a bomb at Hendon. The booking hall at Colindale station was itself destroyed by enemy action in September 1940. On this occasion, a number of passengers on a train which had just arrived at the station were cut by flying glass. For over two hours the crew of the train, aided by others, helped passengers to safety from the train and from the collapsed station buildings and staircase. The same station was hit again only a few days later, when staff had to escort passengers from a damaged train by a somewhat tortuous route to the street.

Serious loss of life and major disruption was caused by a bomb which exploded underground at Balham station on 14th October 1940. LT Museum

The steel-framed construction of Camden Town station saved it from greater damage when it was hit in autumn 1940. LT Museum

Staff were often kept busy dealing with the effects of minor damage – an example is Elephant & Castle, which received an incendiary hit on 7th September 1940. The canopy caught fire but, with the assistance of train staff, the fire was under control within ten minutes and the station saved, although passengers were diverted by way of the Bakerloo station until the integrity of the structure was confirmed. The tunnels themselves, although offering significant security, were not totally safe. The guard of a train at Borough two days after the incident at Elephant reported to the Station Master that he heard "loud reports which shook the tunnel". Following trains ran at reduced speed until inspections confirmed that all was well. The intensity of the raid also caused the Supervisor at Oval to close his station for fear of the welfare of passengers. Disruption on the day in question had been widespread; the service had already been reduced by the cancellation of many trains into service from Highgate following the discovery of an unexploded bomb at Wellington sidings at 6 o'clock in the morning.

This pattern, so early in the blitz, was to be repeated daily for twelve months. Apart from damage from incendiary and high explosive bombs, stations frequently had to close because of dangerous structures nearby or because of flooding – through fire hoses or damaged mains. Cables were also vulnerable to damage, often delaying traffic by disrupting signalling. Everybody was on edge: vigilant neighbours to the line just south of High Barnet reported a hole in the embankment at Sherrards Way, causing much alarm, but is was found to be nothing more sinister than the results of a local dog rooting around for its bone.

And so the story went on, with all sections of the Northern and Northern City Lines suffering damage from time to time and, during the year, virtually all stations on the line suffering some damage – with particular concentrations at London Bridge and at the stations in inner south London.

During the early days of the blitz it was decided to build new deep level shelters on the Northern alignment, with a view to these ultimately forming part of an express post-war line from Golders Green (and possibly Finchley) in the north, by way of Waterloo and Clapham to areas unserved by the Underground in the Southern Railway's territory – Motspur Park and Chessington were in the planners' minds. These grandiose schemes did not reach fruition, but the shelters were built at Belsize Park, Camden Town, Goodge Street, Stockwell, Clapham North, Clapham Common and Clapham South. They were finished by September 1942 and were used initially for military purposes, the enemy's attention having turned away from England for the time being. When the 'V' bomb raids started in 1944 a number were opened to the public for their originally intended purpose. The shelters still exist and are largely used by secure archive companies.

By the time the war was over, staff and passengers alike were weary but jubilant. Trains and other equipment had been run into the ground, maintenance facilities having been put to excellent use to overhaul tanks and manufacture aircraft. The City had been razed and travel patterns had altered enormously. As the crowds celebrated peace in 1945 everybody looked forward to starting again where they had left off in 1939. Events were to prove them wrong.

Opposite **Colindale station, lying close to RAF Hendon and local factories, was particularly vulnerable to enemy action. The original 1924 station building was completely destroyed by a direct bomb hit in September 1940. A temporary wooden ticket hall was constructed which lasted for over 20 years until a new ticket hall was built as part of a large office development.** LT Museum

Nationalisation

With priorities focused on post-war recovery, and steel and other resources in short supply, the once ambitious extensions to the north fell from favour during the early 1950s despite early assurances that all works would be resumed. Quite apart from cost, the fixing of the new green belt boundaries was felt to make further outward expansion redundant, and proposals were progressively abandoned. In 1954 the wholly inadequate steam services to Alexandra Palace were withdrawn, and the fate of that branch was more or less sealed. Main Line freight trains continued from Finsbury Park to Alexandra Palace until 1958, to High Barnet until 1963, and to Edgware (via Mill Hill) until 1964. Once freight had ceased much of the track bed between Highgate, Muswell Hill and Alexandra Palace was sold and building work was underway. From the late 1950s buildings also emerged on the route north of Edgware. Soon afterwards the alignment south of Mill Hill (The Hale) was destroyed by housing and, later, the M1 motorway. The pre-war schemes had withered and died.

Curiously, the ticket system carried on for a while as though the electrification had proceeded. Tickets continued to be available for travel to Mill Hill (the Hale) and Edgware on the local bus (which had taken over this role from the special service) until as recently as the late 1960s, and it was even possible to issue season tickets on this route, though only to a diminishing number of regular holders.

The single track electrification to Mill Hill East never progressed beyond there. This early post-war view shows a 1938 stock train arriving, with the shunting neck for goods trains entering the gasworks from Edgware on the right of the picture. Alan A.Jackson

Scheduled steam services from East Finchley to King's Cross, Moorgate, Finsbury Park and Broad Street ceased in March 1941 following the opening of Highgate Northern Line platforms. Occasional steam railtours, however, continued to visit the line until 1961.
Fred Ivey

The Alexandra Palace service had operated only in peak hours from 1942, with through services beyond Finsbury Park being withdrawn. This diverted most potential traffic to parallel bus services. With the abandonment of the electrification proposals, British Railways, who were responsible for operating the line, successfully proposed closure. The last train ran on 3rd July 1954, the date of this photograph.
Alan A.Jackson

With the stringent restrictions on post-war spending little opportunity existed for heavy capital expenditure and new works were largely confined to patching up war damage and minor improvements. In July 1948 a new interchange subway opened between the Piccadilly and Northern Lines at Leicester Square, to relieve the existing tortuous, heavily used passages, though they were retained also. The Festival of Britain in 1951 spurred improvements at Waterloo where a new bank of three escalators connected the low level concourse to the Festival site from May 1951. When the exhibition closed the escalators were retained, although one was replaced by a stairway when the machine was felt to be more use at Green Park. After temporary closure from 1957 to 1962 the escalator shaft was accommodated in a ticket hall constructed beneath the new Shell building. The Festival of Britain was also the cause of two new escalators at Charing Cross, leading from the ticket hall to the sub-surface concourse below the District Line.

At Hampstead a pair of the old Otis lifts was replaced by two automatic high-speed lifts which came into service on 11th April 1954. This was the second high-speed installation on the line, the first being at Goodge Street in 1937 when three automatic lifts were installed in a shaft previously occupied by two old lifts. At Highgate the moribund workings for the top flight of escalators were revived and a single 'up' escalator was commissioned in August 1957 to carry passengers the further 60 feet from ticket hall level to the Archway Road; for payment of a small toll the escalator was also available for use by pedestrians. The partly built down escalator was abandoned (the machine itself had been commandeered in 1940 for use at Bank to replace war damage). Little other significant building work took place during this period but mention should be made of a new ticket hall at Colindale, opened in 1962, which replaced a temporary structure erected following war damage, and Elephant & Castle where a new station building was provided in 1965 on the existing site, although the old lifts were not superseded until 1983.

Also planned in the 1960s, both Old Street and London Bridge stations were to be subject to major reconstruction and were among the first examples of the post-war rekindling of the improvement of facilities at existing central area stations. On 19th November 1967 London Bridge received a new ticket hall in the main line forecourt linked by escalators to the existing low level passages, the lifts being abolished; as part

In 1958, to improve passenger journey time, two original lifts at Hampstead were replaced by the latest high speed lifts. At stations where traffic levels had not already justified conversion from lift to escalator access, there was also a need by the 1960s to replace the original lift equipment. With almost every lift unique in its length of travel, its equipment space and its ease of access, replacement was a lengthy and expensive exercise.
LT Museum

of a highway scheme Old Street received an enlarged sub-surface ticket hall and a third escalator, the latter being commissioned on 5th December 1971 which then allowed the existing escalators to be modernised.

The train service during the 1950s and 60s was provided entirely by the fleet of 1938 stock. The fleet had been augmented by the addition of 91 cars (known as 1949 stock) which comprised trailers and a new type of car – the Uncoupling Non-Driving Motor (UNDM) which was a non-driving car but with facilities for shunting in depots and yards. These cars were needed to enable a grand sorting out of stock between the Piccadilly, Northern and Bakerloo Lines which created additional trains and mopped up the non-standard formations. The Northern Line allocation was 110 7-car trains, 46 of which included an UNDM car on the 3-car unit instead of a middle driving motor car. During the war years trains were operated as 7-cars all day but from November 1951 uncoupling of trains outside the peaks was re-introduced to save car mileage and both 3-car and 4-car trains operated – the former via the City and the latter via Charing Cross. After the necessary modification of the stock, 'passenger door control' (where passengers could open doors under the overriding supervision of the guard) was introduced in April 1950 in open sections of line. After operating complications became an irritation both uncoupling and passenger door control were abandoned within ten years.

While stations were receiving attention by the late 1960s, all was not well with overall train service levels. In 1969, before the services or the image of the Northern Line had any time to recover, a dispute at the Underground's central overhaul works at Acton cut off the supply of overhauled components, which particularly affected the compressors on 1938 stock trains running on the Northern and Bakerloo Lines. Within weeks up to a third of the Northern service was cancelled and a number of the trains still running had only six cars instead of seven. The level of service was clearly appalling, but the public relations people of the day tried to play the matter down and hardly acknowledged the problems even to commuters with decades of experience. The result of this policy was that the community lost confidence and faith. Action groups were formed – some very powerful and vociferous. Late in the dispute the management became more honest, but it was too late. The damage was done, the line became known as "the Misery Line" and its image was destroyed for years.

The commissioning of Leicester Square Regulating Room, which centralised much control of signalling, allowed a large number of traditional cabins on the line to be closed.
LT Museum

The 1938 stock had never been the most trouble-free although it had given excellent service. Its days by now numbered, by the end of the 1960s thoughts were being given to its replacement. Ordinarily, the Northern could have expected a completely new fleet of trains, but plans were now afoot to extend the Piccadilly Line to Heathrow Airport, justifying a new fleet for that line whose trains were then only a few years old. The planned move entailed the Piccadilly's 1959 stock (with the few units of 1956 and 1962 origin as well) transferring to the Northern with thirty 1938 stock trains being thoroughly refurbished to remain in service to make up the shortfall.

There were worries about the 1938 stock conversions as rehabilitation had always proved both costly and unsuccessful in the past and it was with some relief that London Transport received sanction from its new owners, the Greater London Council, in 1970 to order new trains to top up the anticipated 1959 stock shortfall. It also met both LT's and the GLC's imperative to be seen to be doing something in the face of very poor service and no immediate prospect of 1959 stock transfers. A proportion of new trains would allow the more unreliable old cars to be scrapped and eliminate the various non-standard cars still in evidence, not just on the Northern Line. The sudden urgency for new stock meant there was no time for a new train purpose-designed for the Northern Line and it was therefore decided to purchase 30 new trains based on the Victoria Line 1967 stock design, hastily adapted for two-person operation using some components from scrapped 1938 stock. New trains were obviously welcome, but they were in some ways ill-fitted for the purpose; the control and braking systems (not really designed for manual driving) made things uncomfortable for passengers and the trains never achieved particularly high levels of reliability.

These trains became known as the 1972 Mark I stock, the first of which came into service on 26th June 1972, with the remainder following over the next eighteen months. Each 7-car train consisted of one 3-car and one 4-car unit, all finished in unpainted aluminium alloy. The 4-car units comprised a Motor Car at each end, each with four traction motors, and a pair of trailers in between. The 3-car unit comprised two Motor Cars and a single trailer, however one of these Motor Cars was an UNDM and was similar in principle to the 1949 stock UNDMs whose shunting control cabinets were stripped out for re-use on the new trains. The 1972 stock was notable for its absence of side cab doors, a result of its Victoria Line origins where automatic operation was in use.

Pending the transfer from the Piccadilly Line, authorisation of the then Fleet Line (now the Jubilee) in 1971 gave an opportunity to make further inroads into the ageing 1938 stock fleet, through the early purchase of its first batch of trains – 1972 MkII – for temporary use of the Northern. The 33 trains were of similar (but not identical) design to the MkIs and were operationally compatible. The most obvious difference to passengers was the painting of the passenger doors red; the first of them came into use on 19th November 1973.

Opposite top **For 35 years the 1938 stock was the mainstay of the Northern Line. By the late 1960s however, its increasing age and maintenance requirements, especially when compared with newer rolling stock, had made it costly to operate and thought was given to its replacement. A southbound 1938 stock train is seen at Woodside Park.** John Glover

Opposite **The 1959 stock which was used to assist in the replacement of the Northern Line's 1938 stock owed much to its predecessor's classic design. A train is seen at Euston, City branch, where the station tunnel housed two tracks and an island platform until a new northbound tunnel was built in the mid-1960s.** Capital Transport

For a while over half the fleet was of modern trains, but from 2nd December 1975 onwards 1959 type trains began to transfer, giving the line the additional problem of having three distinct stocks, albeit temporarily. As the 1959 transfers gathered momentum, LT publicly referred to the situation and forecast that with the "nearly new" trains, many of which were now actually at half-life, problems on the Northern would soon be over. It did not work; staff and passengers alike did not perceive 1959s as "nearly new" and claimed that the Northern had been "palmed off again" with other lines' cast-offs. This was not true, although one can forgive memories being too short to recall the arrival of 1938 stock and consequent transfers of older trains to the Central. Further transfers of stock from the Piccadilly completely displaced the 1938 stock, the last service train running on 14th April 1978, although that did not prove to be the end of the story.

Practically, though, the line now had significant new problems. With a reversing loop the Northern is one of the lines which, at any given time, has trains both the 'right' and 'wrong' way round. As the two cannot couple to each other, there is already a loss of flexibility. Now with two stocks this problem is magnified and has led to trains being cancelled through a lack of serviceable stock. By the end of the 1980s the proportions of 1972 and 1959 stock trains rose and fell as policies changed, but ultimately less than 25 per cent of the fleet was left as 1972 stock, some having been converted for use on the Victoria Line, and all of the Mk II fleet working on the Jubilee and then Bakerloo.

Between 1969 and 1976 centralised control was transferred to a purpose-built control room near Euston shared with the Victoria Line. All the remaining signal cabins (except Park Junction used for shunting moves at Highgate depot) were closed. LUL

On the Northern Line of the early 1950s signalling methods had evolved little beyond the system introduced with the opening of the CCE&HR in 1907, although the moving-spectacle signals had given way to two-aspect coloured light signals between the wars, and additional home signals were installed to improve headways. Following experiments with remote control of signal frames, Camden Town was resignalled for control by Interlocking Machines in September 1955. Three machines were provided: one at Mornington Crescent and two at Camden Town itself, one each for the northbound and southbound lines. The machines were under the overriding control of a push button control desk at Camden Town, although for normal purposes the train's route was selected automatically from the coded electrical descriptions passed between the other signal cabins. Clearly there was potential for some staff savings to be had in this area.

A further development was the automatic working of junctions by programme machines, where the timetable was reproduced on a plastic roll in the form of punch holes so that routes were set up 'to programme' and signals cleared accordingly; a refinement was the incorporation of a clock mechanism so that certain train movements could be set up at the specific times required by the timetable. The first installation of programme machines was at Kennington in January 1958 where six machines were introduced. Further programme machines were installed at Camden Town in June and superseded the push button desk and train description control. Euston (City line) followed in November.

To supervise the programme machines a control room was built in a disused lift shaft at Leicester Square, where a track diagram of the whole of the central area of the Northern Line was provided and on which the positions of all trains were indicated. Facilities were provided to monitor the programme machines and to intervene in their operation to route trains by push button control as occasion demanded. In combination with the introduction of a central control room, the little used signal cabins at Charing Cross, London Bridge and Moorgate were closed and modified for remote, push button operation from Leicester Square. In due course the influence of the centralised control room was extended southwards to Morden and northwards to East Finchley. Programme machines were introduced at Archway, East Finchley, Tooting and Morden, and the signal cabin at Clapham Common became remotely controlled from Leicester Square (the sidings and signal cabins at Angel and Stockwell were closed). In 1961 interlocking machines and a push button desk were introduced at Golders Green, which also took over remote control of Hampstead. In 1964/65 programme machines were introduced at Edgware and Colindale, with supervision from Golders Green signal cabin.

When the Victoria Line was opened in 1967 a purpose-built control room was constructed at Cobourg Street (near Euston) and space there was reserved for the future accommodation of the Northern Line control facilities. Between 1969 and 1976 programme machine supervision and centralised control was transferred from Leicester Square and Golders Green control rooms to Cobourg Street, and the signalling at Golders Green, High Barnet and Finchley Central was converted to programme machine control.

Throughout the Northern Line, escalators had been introduced at all stations built after 1907 and had also superseded lifts at most of the busier original stations. A large number of escalators had thus been introduced in the 1920s and 1930s, which meant that by 1970 most of the escalators on the line were becoming life expired. A major programme of escalator modernisation began in 1976 and ten years later the majority of escalators on the line had been superseded by more modern machines. At eleven stations access was still by means of lifts, with in nearly all cases the equipment dating back to the opening of the line in 1907 (and C&SLR lifts modernised in the 1920s largely utilised secondhand ex-LER equipment). Inevitably these lifts, though extremely rugged, were demonstrating their considerable age and a programme of lift replacement began, Angel (in part) and Chalk Farm being the first stations to receive new lift installations, both coming into use in 1979.

Reconstruction work was also necessary on the bridges on the Barnet branch at this time: all were a hundred years old and becoming a liability. Perhaps the most attractive was at Argyle Road, Finchley, which in 1967 became the Underground's first pre-stressed concrete underline bridge. Another 'first' was a bridge of welded box girder construction, rolled into position in April 1970 to carry the railway over the Great North Road at Barnet. This bridge, which had a much longer span than the original, had to be welded on site in conditions designed to be as close as possible to the workshop to ensure consistent quality.

The post-war capital expenditure restrictions (which so far as public transport was concerned drifted on until the 1960s) left a legacy of murky and inefficient stations which were becoming manifestly unattractive. Initially a major programme of relighting stations to higher standards began, replacing tungsten-filament bulbs with fluorescent tubes, most stations being tackled between 1974 and 1980. The new lighting was a partial solution but the harsh fluorescence also drew attention to other signs of antiquity.

During the late 1970s it was realised that passengers placed rather greater weight on an attractive environment than hitherto had been thought. London Transport had been in the fortunate position under Greater London Council control to obtain considerable support for capital expenditure and during a lull in purchases of very expensive new trains decided to switch this support towards a massive programme of station modernisation and refurbishment. Under this programme most stations received at least a coat of paint and general clean up, and the major stations were extensively modernised. In the mid-1980s major work was undertaken at Tottenham Court Road, Leicester Square, Embankment, Waterloo, Goodge Street, Euston and King's Cross, with work planned at other sites. Moorgate and Old Street platforms had already been improved in the late 1960s as part of other schemes and were similar in style to the contemporary Victoria Line. The later programme, however, was based on the revised premise that stations needed their own individual identity, and striking new styles of design were employed.

The arrival of the Victoria Line affected three Northern Line stations. At Euston complete rebuilding was required, the City branch losing its island platform and gaining a new northbound running tunnel and platform. When this opened in 1967 it was hailed as a preview of the new Victoria Line style. This move completed major changes at Euston, which had received a new ticket hall and escalators and lost its lift access as part of the reconstruction of the main line station in the early 1960s (it should be mentioned that both the C&SLR and CCE&HR stations here had closed in 1914, and that both lines had been served by the increasingly cramped and old-fashioned joint ticket hall under the main line concourse until this reconstruction). At Warren Street the Victoria Line did not significantly alter the older parts of the station, although the ticket hall was modernised and a new escalator appeared in the upper flight. At King's Cross, though, the ticket hall was significantly enlarged, although there were no changes at platform level.

The Northern Line platforms at Charing Cross were redecorated as shown here in conjunction with the opening of the Jubilee Line in 1979. Capital Transport

Strand station had seen its Otis lifts improved in 1935 when a form of automatic operation was superimposed, but at the start of the 1970s was otherwise substantially as it was when opened. The construction of the Jubilee Line (at first called the Fleet Line) was to change this dramatically.

Work on the Fleet Line began in 1972 and involved major work at the proposed southern terminus at Charing Cross. One objective of the new scheme was to clear up the irksome turn-of-the-century anomaly whereby the Northern Line's Strand station and the Bakerloo Line's Trafalgar Square station were an almost literal stone's throw away from each other but were otherwise not connected. The new station was therefore planned to absorb Strand and interconnect with Trafalgar Square, the whole complex becoming known as Charing Cross. The new ticket hall incorporated the former Strand sub-surface ticket hall site, but was very considerably extended in area beneath the Strand itself and incorporated new subways to entrances in Villiers Street, Strand (north side) and William IV Street. The existing entrance from the main line station was retained although a single (up) escalator was added.

A major problem arose in providing access from the enlarged ticket hall to the Northern Line platforms immediately below, where the existing service was provided by lifts. The most convenient arrangement of escalators required the upper flight to pass through the existing lift shafts which would have made it difficult to operate the station while the work was being done. The close proximity of Charing Cross (now Embankment) station invited the decision to close Strand station while the reconstruction work was being done, and thus the last train called on 16th June 1973. The reconstructed station came back into service (as Charing Cross) for the opening of the Jubilee Line on 1st May 1979, and on the same day the Northern Line platforms were restored to use and the Bakerloo Line station was renamed and linked to the Northern and Jubilee Lines. The Northern Line platforms had been completely redecorated, the basis being huge murals running the length of the platforms and portraying a design by David Gentleman of the construction of the medieval Charing Cross.

This re-arrangement caused the Northern Line station to revert to the name it had originally borne when it opened in 1907; since the station served Charing Cross main line station it was eminently more appropriate in this guise. However it now became necessary to rename the station of the same name 400 yards to the south. To get passengers used to the new scheme of things Charing Cross [Northern, Bakerloo and District Line station] was renamed Charing Cross (Embankment) on 4th August 1974 and simply Embankment on 9th September 1976.

The last major change to the line was the withdrawal of the services on the Northern City Line on 4th October 1975 in preparation for its adoption by British Rail as part of the Great Northern suburban electrification scheme. Ten months later, the first main-line trains rumbled through from Drayton Park to Moorgate, at the former station using much of the uncompleted 1939 new works which would have linked the line to a new high level Northern Line station at Finsbury Park.

In February 1975 this little branch had seen the Underground's worst peacetime disaster when a morning peak train passed through Moorgate station without stopping and collided with the end of the tunnel: 42 people lost their lives. Following this incident all terminal stations on the Underground were provided with protection to prevent a buffer stop collision at any significant speed.

For many years off-peak services ran from Edgware to Kennington via Charing Cross, High Barnet and Mill Hill East to Morden via Charing Cross; and Golders Green to Morden via Bank (supplemented with extra trains to Morden starting at Euston). From 1967 the Euston reversers were extended initially to Archway, and Golders Green reversers to Colindale. In more recent years Bank trains have been extended to both Mill Hill East and Edgware. Charing Cross services have also been modified; from the late 1960s being enhanced by additional Golders Green–Kennington trains.

During the peak hours trains for many years tended to run to Morden from all northern termini via both routes, except Mill Hill trains always ran via Charing Cross, and most Kennington short workings came from the Edgware branch. That position has changed very little, except that combinations of inevitable short working practices have changed.

In 1966 the Northern lost another idiosyncrasy, in that for the first time Edgware branch trains stopped at Mornington Crescent. Hitherto they had rumbled through without pausing, leaving Barnet services to collect the waiting few.

In the 1970s the loss of leisure traffic was increased by the growth of good suburban restaurants and by the increasingly seedy nature of London's West End. It was no longer either necessary, nor even desirable, to go to town for an evening's entertainment. For those who did brave central London, the earlier scheduling of last trains perpetrated in the 1950s, coupled with the lack of an effective night bus system, made the car a desirable option in case the last train was missed. By 1980 increasing dirt and vagrancy on the Underground made this a most unpalatable option for suburban families and in the outer areas evening trains ran empty. Fortunately, tourism was increasing at the same time and overseas visitors provided crowds where there would otherwise have been under-use. This source of demand can be disturbingly volatile though – in particular in 1985 fears of European terrorism amongst American citizens drastically reduced visitors from across the Atlantic with a noticeable effect on Underground sales.

Commuting patterns were also changing. The reconstruction of the City from the ashes of the war drew additional traffic to that part of the Northern in the late 1950s. More significantly, the peaks were altering shape and by the mid-1980s had become much more broadly spread. Happily, this last few years also saw a huge increase in midday off-peak demand, especially for shopping. This increase was partially due to the granting of free passes to London's senior citizens and partially to the replacement in 1982 of point-to-point season tickets by Travelcards. Our daily commuter could now travel at lunchtime by tube or bus without extra payment.

This freedom, coupled with the buoyancy of London's economy, was to lead to vastly changing fortunes for the Underground. From 1982 onwards, the gentle decline in traffic was transformed into a very vigorous increase. This upsurge, which took most by surprise, led to a completely unpredicted event. The ordering of a second batch of new trains for the Jubilee Line had brought the promise of a cascade of trains around the network, giving the Northern additional 1959 stock (from the Bakerloo Line). Rather than wait for these, it was decided to renovate five withdrawn trains of 1938 stock for operation on the Northern Line. The first of these went into service in September 1986, eight and a half years after the 'last' one had run on the Northern Line and nearly a year after withdrawal from the Bakerloo. Amongst the rather bland trains then running, these veterans were actually quite popular and it was in some ways a shame that enough 1959 trains had been released from the Bakerloo and we had to say a second farewell to the red trains in spring 1988. They were then sold to British Rail for use on the Isle of Wight to replace an earlier generation of trains, a few of which had started work on the Northern Line in 1923.

Among the stations to benefit from GLC-financed modernisation in the mid-1980s was Embankment. A number of central London stations received much-needed refurbishment under this programme. Capital Transport

The Northern Line in Recent Times

On 29th June 1984 the London Transport Executive passed from Greater London Council control to that of the Secretary of State for Transport under the London Regional Transport Act of that year, the body also being restyled London Regional Transport. Under a provision of the Act a subsidiary company was established on 29th March 1985 called London Underground Limited and on 1st April 1985 London Regional Transport's railway activities passed to this subsidiary company.

But today's drive for improvement started in November 1988 with a fundamental change in management practice, turning each line into a business unit headed by a General Manager, instead of the former concept of Divisions responsible solely for operational supervision. Decision making, authority and responsibility were to be devolved from the remote head office to local managers, who had the benefit of being closer to the customer. This move generated tremendous enthusiasm amongst local managers, much of which began to rub off onto staff, without which it is doubtful whether the railway would have survived soaring increases in safety standards without having to endure temporary closures. With this spirit the Underground became the world's first railway to take on a safety management system to recognisable international standards. Alongside this go higher training standards, including the provision of regular refresher training to ensure that staff are prepared for any eventuality. It is recognised that this can be achieved only through effective teamwork, with commitment to safety and service through all levels and functions of the organisation.

Much of the early work of the new organisation had to be devoted to 'behind the scenes' changes, such as recruitment and training, but as the Northern neared its centenary year of 1990 some changes were becoming visible. On stations, work included the provision of improved security and safety, with new alarm systems and the removal of materials – such as laminated panelling – once considered adequately fire safe but now regarded as an unnecessary hazard. This led to many stations reaching 'perpetual building site' status, but the majority of passengers seemed prepared to endure temporary difficulty for long-term improvement.

Amongst the more controversial innovations of the later 1980s was the implementation of the Underground Ticketing System (UTS), including the replacement of all ticket offices with modern integrated facilities. The self-service ticket machines went down quite well but the ticket gates caused much initial emotion until people got used to them, and found that the throughput of a batch of gates was much greater than conventional ticket barriers. Slightly earlier the Northern had benefited from two major improvements in the provision of information. Visually, dot-matrix train indicators were provided on most platforms to provide estimated arrival times for the next three trains. The Northern was the first line to receive this equipment, but there were many teething problems, not least the famous Northern Line 84-second minute, which needed addressing.

Parallel improvements in audible information on stations came with the

At six stations at the south end of the line, Station Focal Points have been created. These highly visible rooms for staff also house television monitors and video-recording facilities and are linked to remote help points in all parts of the station. Although used normally for information, the deterrent value of the facilities has helped considerably in cutting crime rates.

development of a centralised public address system, although again by the end of the 1980s some fundamental design faults were becoming evident. Despite these problems, the passenger today is much better informed of what is happening than at any time in the railway's history.

The south end of the line had developed an unenviable reputation for crime. Although absolute figures were not high when compared with street crime there was no doubt that the area around Tooting and Clapham had the highest crime rates of the Underground. In 1985 the policing of the area was increased and a number of closed circuit television (CCTV) cameras installed. Over the following two years this had the effect of halving assaults and pickpocketing. In 1987 it was decided to intensify the campaign and staff at six stations in the area were increased and became more visible. 'Focal points' were established, where a supervisor could see what was going on and be seen by the customer, who now had an information facility as well. From the focal point the staff could monitor virtually all parts of the station by CCTV and there was continuous recording of the output of all cameras. Passengers anywhere on the station were within easy reach of a help point which could be used either to obtain information or to raise the alarm in the event of emergency. Any emergency call not answered promptly by local staff was passed straight through to the Police Information Room.

The further success of this scheme was considerable. The scheme benefited from a dedicated team of staff and from warm co-operation between the staff and the local police offices. A programme of 'surgeries', where staff and police would meet passengers, was started with excellent feedback from all concerned. Crime rates fell still further; there was even some evidence that evening traffic, always the most threatened, was increasing again. The way was clear for the scheme to be extended to other stations, ultimately across the Underground.

Other improvements also began to show. Cleaning standards were increased at nearly all stations, to the extent that passengers actually started to comment on them. This was matched by intensive cleaning of the trains themselves – initially behind the scenes to remove potentially flammable accumulations – and then through the saloons. Again, favourable comment was forthcoming. The changes were helped during autumn

1989 by the replacement of the trains' old brake blocks by new materials which wore much more slowly and thus deposited far less dust (a reduction of some 60 per cent), coupled with a resumption of regular cleaning of station fluorescent lighting tubes abandoned some years earlier. The result was clearly visible. In November 1989 the campaign was rounded off by the initiation of litter removal from trains during the day at the main termini. The immediate result was the collection of 15-20 sacks of rubbish daily, which hitherto had been carried about the line all day – an unsightly and hazardous mess.

Following the serious and tragic escalator fire at King's Cross in 1987, the perceived need to call the fire brigade to any suspected incident, however small (even the mildest smell of smoke), became very disruptive from 1988, given the brigade's duty to be satisfied that any fire was out. Over the years the Northern's tunnels had become ingrained with generations of dust and grease – never in great accumulation, but given that most tunnels had seen two to three hundred trains pass each day, every day for decades, some deposit was inevitable. It is very easy for a stray spark from a collector shoe to ignite this deposit, or litter, and start a small fire. For this reason, litter removal in tunnels was stepped up and this was followed by the start of an intensive and laborious cleaning of the trackside, including the ballast laid between the rails.

Efforts were also needed on the trains to go beyond cleaning regimes and provide interiors which could take full advantage of the fire-safe materials now available, whilst at the same time giving a brighter and more comfortable ride. Although the 1959 stock had insufficient life left to justify a complete refit, work started in 1989 on replacing ceilings and installing public address and passenger alarm facilities, to bring them into line with current safety expectations. As trains were overhauled they were also given brighter interiors to provide a reasonable appearance for the remaining years. Plans also existed for comprehensive refitting of the later 1972 stock trains from 1992, but these were not implemented in the light of a mounting possibility that the Northern Line would soon get new trains.

Major improvements to the train service are hindered by the complexity of the Line's junctions and the limitations of the signalling control system. In spite of the efforts of local management, by 1990 it had become clear that comprehensive improvement was essential. But the degree of regularity and reliability which was clearly demanded could not be provided with trains at the end of their working life, and with signalling, control and power supply systems dating in part back to the 1920s. Matters had been compounded by successive additions of more recent equipment which mixed a wide range of technologies and created difficulties at the interfaces. Thoughts began to turn to major replacement of infrastructure which could address these issues together. Furthermore usage of the line was increasing and it appeared the demand could outstrip the service levels being offered, further increasing overall unreliability. With new signalling and trains it could increase its capacity by 30 per cent in some areas, making full use of the currently under-utilised (and highly expensive) track and tunnels. This would justify change by itself: in practice the City branch of the Northern was perceiving some exceptional demand increases. It connects with both the Docklands Light Railway and the extended Jubilee Line serving London's new Docklands. It also serves the areas both north and south of the Square Mile which offer an explosion in office developments, and the proposed major international terminal for cross-Channel traffic at St Pancras, with the massive new interchange at King's Cross, now being contemplated. There are other development sites too (both north of King's Cross station itself and at Mornington Crescent).

Although a number of 1959 stock trains received various experimental coloured interiors in order to brighten them up, most of the trains retained the familiar grey finish until the end.
Capital Transport

By 1990 the bulk of the Northern Line's trains were thirty years old, and much of the signalling and control systems of a similar age. There was an obvious appeal for an approach called the 'Total Modernisation' concept, where trains, signalling and control equipment would be replaced simultaneously, together with key track improvements. The advantage of this approach was that maximum benefit could be achieved from introducing all the features together – principally the necessary changes in service frequency and reliability, with automatic operation implied using the latest 'moving block' technology. But there was a down-side, about to become all too evident on the Central Line where total line modernisation was then being implemented. This was the phenomenal cost, compounded by a significant increase in unreliability during implementation. It was not just the cost – more importantly it was the commitment to an enormous proportion of the Underground's overall expenditure (the funding of which it has little control over) for so long a period of time and at the expense of other pressing demands. Although a project team was established the Underground felt unable to enter into such commitments, particularly until such time as the Central Line modernisation was out of the way. Excepting preliminary work, the matter was temporarily shelved.

As part of the Northern Line's centenary celebrations a train of 1959 stock was painted in a 1920's livery. Alongside is a 1972 stock train externally finished in the newest livery, the only one of these trains on the line to be so treated.
James Blake

Although lengthened in 1924, the island platform at Angel was little changed from 1901. This view shows how narrow it was; quite unable to cope safely with the recent increases in traffic at this station. Capital Transport

By the beginning of 1990 work was under way for a totally new £70m station at Angel, to replace the cramped surface building and inadequate island platform. A new northbound platform and short diversion tunnels were built to the south-west of the existing island platform, which was retained in the form of a very wide but otherwise normal "side" platform (widened across the old northbound trackbed) to serve the southbound line. A new concourse between the platforms leads to a flight of escalators – the longest on the system – and these in turn lead to a new ticket hall site in Upper Street. The old station closed completely after traffic on Friday 7th August 1992 and during the weekend arrangements were made to effect the diversion of the northbound line, which was completed by 18.00 on Sunday 9th August. The new station building and northbound platform were intended to open at the same time, but difficulties in commissioning the new escalators meant some delay; the northbound platform came briefly into use in the afternoon of Wednesday 15th August (but closed the following day) and did not properly come into use until 17th September. It had always been the intention to keep closed the southbound platform until the widening and modernisation work had been substantially completed; the platform, now linked to the new lower concourse, was reopened in October, and finishing works were completed by spring 1993.

This photo is taken from a similar point to the one to its left and shows the massive improvement possible at Angel following diversion of the northbound line to a new platform. Capital Transport

The Northern Line northbound platform at the busy interchange station at Bank, modernisation of which was completed in 1998.
Capital Transport

The way to new trains came in 1993 with the Government's launch of the Private Finance Initiative, designed to introduce private sector money into public sector organisations. A complex tendering process resulted in contracts being placed with GEC Alsthom (now Alstom) for the provision of new trains and all train maintenance. The value of the trains was to be over £400m, with the contractor financing, designing, building and operating for 20 years the resulting fleet. The Underground were to pay GEC a sum thought likely to be in the region of £40-£45 million a year for the provision of the train fleet, but would not own the trains or the maintenance facilities. The LUL payments to Alstom are performance based, and are designed to maximise the customer offering whilst avoiding taking the usual engineering and maintenance risks in-house. The contract was signed on 8th December 1994, and the 170 resident depot staff at Morden and Golders Green were transferred to Alstom from 26th November 1995, that company taking a lease on the premises and equipment preparatory to the arrival of the new trains; the old stock remained in LUL ownership until disposal.

Components for the trains have been sourced from around the world, and the body shells come from Spain. Complications arose at the assembly plant in Birmingham, and it was announced in November 1996 that the trains would enter service around a year late, though it was hoped that the later deliveries could be accelerated to complete the

A train of 1995 stock at Golders Green. The design is almost identical to the 1996 stock on the Jubilee Line. Capital Transport

overall programme on time. Three months in advance of the next, the first train was delivered on 20th December 1996 following which an intensive programme of testing and gauging was embarked upon. Entry into passenger service took place in July 1998.

The 106 new trains are designed to operate in 6-car formations and are not dissimilar to those built for the Jubilee Line. There are 248 seats on each train including 48 tip-up seats which, when folded away, provide space for four wheelchairs in each car, compared with 288 seats on a 1959 stock train and 268 on the 1972 stock. The reduction in seating reflects the shorter trains as well as a slight increase in circulating space per car. Ventilation has been improved and audible and visual information is provided throughout the train. The trains are designed to be safer than any so far, with improved emergency evacuation facilities bringing new standards to the Underground.

Some additional siding accommodation has been built at Edgware, Highgate, High Barnet and Morden, partly to increase stabling accommodation, and partly to improve flexibility. The money is not yet available to undertake the complete replacement of the signalling and control systems, but Alstom is supplying new plant in the depots, new train radio and CCTV equipment. Substations have been replaced or upgraded to allow for the improved service levels and the regenerative braking system, which returns traction current to the track during the braking process for use by other trains.

interior view of the latest Northern Line rolling stock. The line colour is incorporated in the seating moquette pattern and on the armrests. Capital Transport

Clapham Common is one of two remaining sub-surface island platforms on the line, the other being neighbouring Clapham North. Rebuilding of this station is currently under consideration. Capital Transport

Whilst the Angel development was proceeding Parliamentary powers were sought for very significant extensions to London Bridge and Tottenham Court Road stations. Expansion of the latter station was not pursued in the light of the non-progress of the Chelsea-Hackney and Crossrail schemes, both of which were planned to serve that station, but in 1998 work started on a revised scheme to provide new escalators and a larger ticket hall. At London Bridge comprehensive changes were required to alleviate the mounting capacity problems and to accommodate the Jubilee Line. The changes were in some ways similar to those at Angel, with a new platform being built on a short diversion tunnel. This time, however, it was the southbound platform which was diverted, and the old southbound platform tunnel was converted into a central passenger concourse. The 1967 ticket hall and escalators were retained, though the ticket hall was somewhat enlarged and further escalators leading to a new ticket hall were introduced. Subways to the new Jubilee Line platforms were added at low level. The new platform came into use on 20th October 1996. Also in connection with the Jubilee Line extension, major work took place at Waterloo between 1997 and 1999. Major capacity increases are also being considered for Camden Town. Long term plans exist for the rebuilding of Clapham North and Clapham Common, being the only remaining narrow island platform stations of the old City & South London pattern after the rebuilding of Angel. In the suburbs changes are planned for some stations to provide step-free access between street and platforms.

The Northern Line has thus developed from its pioneering beginnings to one of the

This listed structure is the 1924 entrance to Clapham Common station, a new ticket hall having been built beneath the roadway. Capital Transport

Mornington Crescent station closed for renovation and new lift works in October 1992 but because of financial difficulties did not re-open until 27th April 1998. This view shows a refurbished platform. Capital Transport

largest of the deep level tube lines. It incorporates the longest tunnel on the London Underground, 17¼ miles from Morden to East Finchley via the City; until recently this was the longest railway tunnel in the world. The confidence of the promoters of the old City & South London Railway in an age when even electric light was something of a novelty can only be admired, but it is doubtful even if they could have foreseen the impact that their little railway was to have in spawning new schemes and hence in moulding the future shape of London. Most passengers simply use the line to get from one place to another without a thought for how struggling miners toiled in unbearable conditions to build this, adapt that or reconstruct the other. Nor are they worried about how it was that engineers, probably working by the light of oil lamps, over a hundred years ago managed to build tunnels from different points in London which months later would meet within an inch.

Oval station received smart new cladding and a canopy in 1998, together with retiling of the concourse leading to the escalators with an appropriate cricketing theme. Capital Transport